What Life Is Meant to Be Like

Also by Ross West

Understanding the Gospel of Matthew

Understanding the Gospel of Mark

Understanding the Gospel of Luke

Understanding the Gospel of John

Understanding the Book of Acts

Understanding 1 Corinthians

Understanding 2 Corinthians

Understanding the Letter to the Galatians

Understanding the Letter to the Ephesians

Understanding the Letter to the Philippians

Understanding the Letters to the Colossians and Philemon

Understanding 1 and 2 Thessalonians

Understanding the Book of Hebrews

Understanding the Book of James

Understanding 1, 2, and 3 John

Understanding the Book of Revelation

Reading the Bible Jesus Read

Grief and Hope

Seven Words to Live By

The Christmas to Remember

Guidance for a Good Life

Living in the Meanwhile

*How to Be Happier in the Job
You Sometimes Can't Stand*

Go to Work and Take Your Faith Too!

Teaching Adults the Bible (co-author)

What Life Is Meant to Be Like

Meditations on Scripture Texts
from the Revised Common Lectionary
Year B

Second Edition

By Ross West

Positive Difference Communications
Dallas, Texas

What Life Is Meant to Be Like:
Meditations on Scripture Texts
from the Revised Common Lectionary Year B
Second Edition

Copyright © 2017, 2021 by Ross West
All rights reserved.

Dewey Decimal Classification 252
Subject Heading: SERMONS

Contents

Tenth Sunday after Pentecost

Introduction

These meditations follow the Revised Common Lectionary for Year B. (*Guidance for a Good Life: Meditations on Scripture Texts from the Revised Common Lectionary Year A* and *Living in the Meanwhile: Meditations on Scripture Texts from the Revised Common Lectionary Year C* are also available.) The lectionary texts are meant to provide substance and direction for following the Christian year. More and more pastors—even some Baptists, which I am—use the lectionary to guide choices for Scripture texts and thus lead their churches in a balanced look at Scripture over a three-year period of time.[1]

These meditations are also indexed by Scripture text to provide convenient access to the texts from the various Bible books. The index should be especially helpful if you do not use the lectionary and/or you simply are looking for a meditation on a specific Bible book or text.

This second edition has been expanded from the previous edition with additional meditations. It is thus about a third larger than the previous edition.

–Ross West, D.Min.

1.

Isaiah 40:1-11
On Tiptoe for Christmas
Second Sunday of Advent

When was the last time you stood on tiptoe? Or, when was the last time you stood on tiptoe figuratively speaking, in anticipation of something to which you were looking forward? Children won't have to think back very far to find an answer. If you are young at heart if not in years, you will not have to think back very far either.

Children know how to stand on tiptoe. They are beginning to stand on tiptoe now, for Christmas. They are yearning for a glimpse of Christmas. They know it is just around the corner, and they can hardly wait. They have mastered the art of anticipating Christmas. This season is filled with wonder for them, and it is filled with wonder for all who still know how to stand on tiptoe.

It could be, though, that some of us have just about forgotten what anticipation and wonder and standing on tiptoe are all about. Maybe we think there's nothing much new left anymore. Maybe we think there's no more adventure ahead.

And, even if there were, we've simply got too many things to do to be going on an adventure.

Every person, though, needs a sense of wonder, of anticipation, of expectancy as Christmas approaches. That's at least a part of what the text from Isaiah is about. In Isaiah 40, the inspired prophet was standing on tiptoe for Christmas. From the vantage point of more than 500 years before Christ, he was looking forward to Christmas.

The immediate reference of these verses was to the return of the Israelites from exile in Babylon. They were being allowed to return to the freedom and joy of life in their own city, Jerusalem.

These verses tell also, though, of the prophet's longing for the Messiah. The prophet stood on tiptoe, looking forward to that time when the way of the Lord would be prepared, truly, and then when the glory of the Lord would be revealed and all flesh—everybody—would see it.

From the first century on, Christians have believed that this prophet was standing on tiptoe for the coming of Christ. The prophet who wrote Isaiah 40 was standing on tiptoe for this event, Christmas. Let's stand on tiptoe ourselves for a bit and think about what it means for us.

Standing on Tiptoe to See Better

Why do people stand on tiptoe, anyway? The answer is simple. People stand on tiptoe in order to see. Some need or interest calls a person to stand on tiptoe in order to see better or farther.

The person wants to get a better glimpse of whatever it is he or she is trying to see.

That reality is why Christmas calls us to stand on tiptoe. We need to be able to see it better. We need to rise above where we are in order to get a better glimpse of Christmas.

Something in our hearts makes us long for Christ. As Augustine said centuries ago, people's hearts are restless until they find rest in Christ. This need in our hearts calls on us to stand on tiptoe for Christmas, to see as did the shepherds this thing that has come to pass.

On our own and in our present circumstances, we may not be able to see Christmas very well. Christmas calls us to rise above where we are in order to see Christmas better.

Standing on Tiptoe
to See Something Truly Important

People do not stand on tiptoe for just anything. They stand on tiptoe in order to see something important.

We need to stand on tiptoe in this season to see something truly important—the birth of "a Savior, who is the Messiah, the Lord," as the angels told the shepherds (Luke 2:11). Christmas is about something truly important. It is about Jesus, our Savior, who came to redeem people from the penalty and power of sin and to call us to follow him in service and abundant living. Jesus has come to be with us and to call us to live life in the best possible way.

Christmas is God's supreme effort to get through to people with God's message. It is worth standing on tiptoe to see.

A woman and her small child were looking at a picture of Jesus. The mother asked, *Do you know who this is?* The child replied, *It's a picture of God.* The mother at first wanted to correct the child, to tell her, *No, that's not a picture of God. You can't see God. It's a picture of Jesus.* Wisely, though, she didn't say that. Later, talking to a friend about the incident, the mother said, *My child said more than she realized she was saying. When she saw Jesus, she truly saw God.*

A man stood trying to see what was painted on the ceiling of a church in Europe. He could not quite make it out. Then someone put a mirror into his hand. He directed the mirror toward the ceiling, looked down into the mirror, and then was able to see the beautiful paintings high above him. Jesus is the mirror God has placed in our hands in order that we might be able to see what God is like.

Christmas is important because it is about Jesus, God's Son. Christmas is worth standing on tiptoe for.

Standing on Tiptoe Because It's Fun and Joyful

There is another reason to stand on tiptoe for Christmas, anticipating its coming. Because it's fun, because of the joy that is in Christmas. The joy that is in Christmas makes standing on tiptoe an exercise filled with fun and joy. Christmas means having that for which we really yearn, way down deep inside. There is joy in anticipating something like that.

We can catch that note of joy in Isaiah 40. Verse 9 exults, "Get you up to a high mountain, O Zion, herald of good tidings; lift up your voice with strength, O Jerusalem, herald of good tidings, lift it up, do not fear; say to the cities of Judah, 'Here is your God!'" It's a time of good things and good news!

This joy is at the heart of Christmas, and it makes standing on tiptoe for Christmas necessary and desirable. In Christ, every person can know freedom, redemption, salvation, and new life. In Christ, every person has more possibilities for growth, for life abundant, than he or she ever dreamed possible. There is joy in standing on tiptoe for such an event.

Are you on tiptoe for Christmas? Children are. You can do that, too. Come like a child. Stand on tiptoe. Trust me. You can see much better. You can see Jesus. You can know the joy that is at the heart of Christmas. "O come let us adore Him, Christ the Lord."[2]

2.

Ephesians 1:3-14
What God Is Up To

Second Sunday after Christmas Day

A young person said, *I don't know why I am here! I've got to know before I can go on.*

Really? Probably not. But all of us, no matter our age, would like to know why we are here, wouldn't we? Plus, it would help us greatly in living life if we did. We'd like to know what life is all about and where we fit in. We feel that if we had at least an inkling of the purpose of it all, we could live with more purpose ourselves.

The Christian faith opens the door to finding our way to this purpose. In fact, the Christian faith insists that there is a purpose to life, that life does make sense, and that we can indeed fit in. From eternity to here and beyond, God has been and is up to something—something wonderful, something important, and something with personal meaning for us.

The text from Ephesians puts it into words. These words both show us the big picture and make them personal for us. They further call us to make God's purpose our own and show us how to do it.

God Is Creating a People Who Will Truly Belong to Him and Relate Faithfully to Him

Our universe is vast. Current estimates are that there are at least 100 billion galaxies in the universe,[3] with each galaxy having perhaps 100 million stars in it.[4] Our own galaxy may have hundreds of billions of stars in it.[5]

Through a process science is leading us to discover, we know that God made them all. Yet Scripture says that God takes note when a small bird falls to the ground (Matthew 10:29-30). The message of Scripture is that God is concerned for the universe and for the smallest creature.

But God's prime interest seems to be in people. Psalm 8 asks, "What are human beings that you are mindful of them, mortals that you care for them? (Psalm 8:4). The next verse continues, "Yet you have made them a little lower than God, and crowned them with glory and honor" (Ps. 8:5).

God gave us freedom to accept God's view of us and respond to him, or not. God yearns for people to be his own, to belong to him, but we have the choice. The focus of Scripture is on this prime purpose of God, to create a people who will truly belong to him and relate faithfully to him.

Ephesians 1:4-5 speaks of how God has chosen us to belong to him. ". . . He chose us in Christ before the foundation of the world to be holy and blameless before him in love. He destined us for adoption as his children through

Jesus Christ, according to the good pleasure of his will." Whatever else these verses mean, they mean that God wants us for his own. He wants us to belong to him and to relate faithfully to him.

None of us is an accident. We were made to fit in God's purpose. None of us is a misfit. We were made to fit in just the right place, in the place for which God chose us.

These verses are not talking about fate but about God. In love God shaped us to fit in a just-right place among the people whom God is creating. The fact of God's choice of us means that you and I have a purpose in life.

So what is that purpose? God chose us to belong to him, first of all. What we are and what we do beyond that is secondary. Any achievements and occupations are transitory. Belonging to God is eternal. Of course, we have tasks to do, but these tasks grow out of our belonging to God. Our purpose in life is to be God's people, "holy and blameless before him in love" (Eph. 1:4).

When a parent holds the newborn baby, is the parent thinking, *Oh, I'm holding a doctor or a lawyer or something else we might think is magnificent?* Of course, the parent—or more likely, a grandparent—might joke about it. But to say it seriously would be an unusual thought, wouldn't it? Certainly every parent has hopes and dreams for his or her child, and parents want to help their children identify and reach their dreams. But when the parent is holding that little baby, he or she most likely is thinking, *This is my baby. I love this baby so much.*

That is how God feels about us, I believe. Of prime importance is that we belong to God.

That's what we might call the human side of God's choice—God's concern for us. The other side we might call the divine side of God's choice. God chose us so that God himself might be praised. It was for "the praise of his glorious grace that he freely bestowed on us in the Beloved" (1:6). Our very existence and our participation in God's purpose are meant to bring praise to God.

So what is God up to? It's risky to try to summarize a response to such a big question in a single sentence, but try this: *God is up to creating a people who will truly belong to him—including you and me—thus bringing praise to him.* That's what God is up to.

This means that you and I are not alone in the vastness of the universe. It further means that when we belong to God our lives cannot be wasted. We matter and can matter much in the overall picture of God's purpose.

How God Is Doing This

That's what God is up to. *God is up to creating a people who will truly belong to him—including you and me—thus bringing praise to him.*

How is God doing it? God is creating this people through Christ.

The thoughts of this passage in Ephesians show us the importance of Christ. Christ is the instrument through whom God is creating this people who will belong to him. That is why God took such trouble in preparing for the coming of Christ. That is the reason Christ relinquished the place of honor and majesty to become incarnate and even submitted to death.

"In him"—in Christ—"we have redemption through his blood, the forgiveness of our trespasses, according to the riches of his grace that he lavished on us" (1:7). What God has done in Christ shows us the length to which God would go to create a people who would belong to him. What God has done in Christ shows us also how far away from God we were that God would have to do such a thing.

Through Christ's redemptive death, we have been adopted as children, members of God's own family. We have been redeemed—bought back out of slavery—to become again God's children.

The magnificent movie, *Twelve Years a Slave*, won the academy award for best picture in 2014.[6] The movie shows in terrible detail the evils of slavery. It shows, too, the contrast between slavery and freedom. The slave named Solomon was at last freed as a result of the actions of a person who put his life at risk to save him. In that act we have a small picture of the gospel in action.

What is God up to? God is creating a chosen people who will be his and will bring praise to him. God is doing this through Christ, who died "to bring you to God," as 1 Peter 3:18 puts it.

How We Enter Into God's Purpose

But how do we enter into this purpose that God is accomplishing through Christ? Verse 13 states, "In him you also, when you had heard the word of truth, the gospel of your salvation, and had believed in him, were marked with the seal of the promised Holy Spirit."

We must hear "the word of truth" with understanding. That means we must pay attention to this word.

Let us recognize with sympathy and love that some have more difficulty hearing this message than do others. Some have spent their lives in difficult situations, and their difficulties have drowned out the message of what God has done in Christ. Some have not heard the gospel preached faithfully; they have heard it only as it has been distorted by the surrounding culture.

Back to that movie—*Twelve Years a Slave.* In the movie, the slaves heard Scripture preached by their white masters, but how distorted the message was, preached in the context of the justification of the cruelties of slavery.

Some people in our own day hear only a politicized version of the gospel, a gospel that requires adherence to certain political views or certain cultural views. How hard it is for anyone to get through to the gospel's heart in such a situation. But the prayer is that we will proclaim the gospel of God's grace clearly and lovingly and that people will have the opportunity to hear this "word of truth" with understanding.

Further, we must respond to this "word of truth" with commitment. Verse 13 describes the recipients of this letter as having "believed in him." That is, they believed in Christ, whom we recall is God's instrument in creating a people who will belong to him. What does *believing in him* mean? It's more, much more, than intellectual assent that God exists. It's trusting our whole lives to God.

When we do trust our lives to God, God acts in a mighty way. God puts his "seal," God's stamp of ownership, on us.

How does God do that? He does that by giving us the Holy Spirit God had promised (1:13). This stamp of ownership is the guarantee that we will be completely, fully redeemed, that we will fully and completely belong to God although now we may be tugged in different directions.

These verses in Ephesians, verses 3-14 of chapter 1, put in a nutshell what God is up to and show us our personal place in it. These verses show us what God is up to.

But now, what are we up to? Unless we are up to what God is up to we will miss much that is truly important in life. It's up to us to hear this "word of truth" and respond to it in faith with our very lives.

3.
1 Samuel 3:1-20
Listening
Second Sunday after the Epiphany

Listening, truly listening, to a person may well be the greatest act of respect for that person. That's a truism that rings true with our experience, doesn't it? We know what it is like to realize that a person is not listening, not truly listening, to us. What generally we want most from other people is for them to truly see us and to listen to us so that they know who we are and how we wish to be understood, valued, and respected. Much of our dissatisfaction with other people, including groups of which we are a part, including perhaps even our church, is that we feel that others do not truly see us, do not listen to us, and thus do not value who we are.

Could such thoughts apply to our relationship to God as well? This passage calls us to think about that.

Steven Spielberg is, of course, the renowned director of many wonderful movies that are a part of our heritage—*Jaws, Close Encounters of the Third Kind, Raiders of the Lost Ark, E.T., Schindler's List, Saving Private Ryan,* and many others.[7] His creative work has made him

29

legendary. He was being interviewed some years ago on the television show *Inside the Actor's Theatre*. On this show, the interviewer closed each interview by asking a list of ten questions. One of the questions was, "When you enter heaven, if there is a heaven, what do you hope to hear God say?" When the interviewer asked this question of Spielberg, he replied, "Thanks for listening." Spielberg then explained by calling attention to Deuteronomy 6:4, which begins a treasured Scripture passage with the words, "Hear, O Israel." The Hebrew word *shema* is translated "hear," but it actually means more than simply hearing the sound. It means *listen*. God was saying, *Listen, O Israel*. So God says to us, *Listen*.

That word *shema*, meaning *listen*, appears often in this passage in 1 Samuel 3. That's what this passage in 1 Samuel 3 is about, in fact— listening. As we read and consider the passage, we'll understand it best if we recognize that it is first of all about listening, especially to God, who wants us to know him and who he is even more than we want other people to listen to us and value us. We'll also find in this story of a child some clues about how we might truly listen.

First, a bit of background. The final verse of the Book of Judges describes the overall scene of Israel's life in that day. It reads like this: "In those days there was no king in Israel; all the people did what was right in their own eyes" (Judges 21:25).

That was so in all Israel, and it was even so in the household of Eli, the priest. Verses 12-13 of 1 Samuel 2 state the situation bluntly: "Now the sons of Eli were scoundrels; they had no regard for the LORD or for the duties of the priests to the people."

Verses 13-17 of chapter 2 tell one way in which the sons sinned against the Lord and the people. They were engaged in priestly service under their father, Eli. In this service, they actually stole from the Lord and the people in the way they handled the offerings of sacrificial animals. As the latter part of verse 17 states, " . . . They treated the offerings of the LORD with contempt." Eli's sons were "fattening" themselves, and their father Eli was at least to a degree complicit in what they were doing with the offerings (1 Samuel 2:27-29). He "did not restrain them" (1 Sam. 3:13).

Eli's sons also "lay with the women who served at the entrance to the tent of meeting" (2:22). Eli warned them about their bad behavior, but he was unable to stop them. "They would not listen to the voice of their father" (2:25). Note that statement: "They would not listen." Because they would not listen, their days were numbered. But they didn't even know that word of warning, for they weren't listening.

Of course, the main character in all that was happening was a boy named Samuel. His mother, Hannah, had given birth to him miraculously. His birth to Elkanah and Hannah took place in the normal way, but it was an answer to Hannah's fervent prayer. As part of her prayer to at last have a child, Hannah had promised to rear the child as a nazirite, in essence by following certain religious practices. Part of her commitment

31

evidently also was to allow the child to be raised by the priest Eli. The little boy would serve in the worship center at Shiloh under the guidance of Eli, the priest. Samuel's mother came to see him each year and brought him "a little robe" (2:19). So she continued to care for him.

Living in a Spiritual Desert (3:1)

"The boy Samuel was ministering to the LORD before Eli" (3:1). As we have seen in the behavior of Eli and his two wayward sons, it was a time of spiritual dryness. As the rest of the verse states, "The word of the LORD was rare in those days; visions were not widespread." Given what we know of the situation, why do you suppose that was? Most likely it was because the people, even those who were the religious leaders, were not receptive. They were involved with other things. They weren't paying attention. How quickly they had forgotten how they had gotten to the Promised Land. They had forgotten the Lord's care for them on the journey and then his deliverance over and over during the time of the judges.

Do you recall Holman Hunt's painting of Jesus knocking at the door, seeking entrance? It's called "The Light of the World," and the larger version is in St. Paul's Cathedral in London. I was delighted to see it in person a few years ago.[8] There's a story of a child viewing the painting with her parents. As the child and her parents looked at the painting, she asked, *Why don't the people open the door to Jesus?* And then, before the parents could answer, as sometimes happens with children, she answered her question herself. She said, *Maybe they're not at home, or maybe they're not paying attention because they're doing other things, or maybe the television is on so loud that they cannot hear the knock.*

So as we think about the situation with Eli, his boys, and their fellow Israelites, perhaps the question to ask at first is, *What were they listening to so that they were not paying attention to God's message?* The question is for us, too, isn't it? *What are we listening to that prevents our listening to God and paying attention to what God is saying to us?*

Hearing and Beginning to Listen (3:2-9)

The story of the boy Samuel's hearing words but not recognizing who was speaking is a treasure, of course. It indicates the dawning of Samuel's consciousness of a personal experience with God.

The text doesn't indicate specifically how old the boy was. The word translated "boy" can represent a range of ages, from a child to a youth and even to a young adult.[9] A tradition says he was almost twelve, the age at which a Jewish boy was to take responsibility for his own spiritual growth.

Samuel heard the voice say his name. He thought the voice was Eli's, and so Samuel went to Eli to hear what Eli had to say. This happened three times. Verse 7 explains about Samuel, "Now Samuel did not yet know the LORD, and the word of the LORD had not yet been revealed to him." It was not that Samuel was completely ignorant of

33

God. He would have learned much about God from Eli. The idea rather was that Samuel had not *experienced* God for himself. He had certainly not experienced God in the way he was about to experience God more directly.[10]

In spite of Eli's wrongs, Eli was still spiritually perceptive. He "discerned that the LORD was calling the boy" (3:8, NASB). He then instructed Samuel about what to do if it happened again. Samuel was to say to the Voice, "Speak, LORD, for your servant is listening" (3:9).

Listening to a Hard Message to Hear (3:10-14)

The Voice did speak again. Samuel listened. The message was hard to hear. The message was about judgment on Eli and his family.

In Samuel's encounter with God, we see a couple of characteristics of what generally happened with prophets in the Old Testament. Most importantly, first they listened to God. As Jeremiah 23:18 suggests, the first responsibility of a prophet is to stand "in the council of the LORD so as to see and to hear his word." Second, what prophets heard as they listened to the Lord was generally bad news, hard to hear and hard to talk about. Read just a little of the prophets—like the call of Isaiah in Isaiah 6 and the call of Jeremiah in Jeremiah 1—and you'll see that rather clearly.

Samuel had heard the bad news from the Lord. Would Samuel talk about it? God had a job, a hard job, for Samuel to do. Would Samuel do it?

Telling the News from God (3:15-18)

Because of the nature of God's message to Samuel, Eli had to pry it out of Samuel. At last, "Samuel told him everything and hid nothing from him" (1 Sam. 3:18).

Samuel was fulfilling the second duty of a prophet. The first duty was to listen to God. The second was to tell others what God said—the truth, the whole truth, and nothing but the truth, even if the truth was bad news, the news of judgment.

Preview of the Rest of Samuel's Story (3:19-20)

This experience with God in the night was the beginning for Samuel. Look where it took him and what God made of this little boy. "Thus Samuel grew and the LORD was with him and let none of his words fail. All Israel from Dan even to Beersheba knew that Samuel was confirmed as a prophet of the LORD" (3:20, NASB).

Learning to Listen to God

So what do we learn from Samuel, especially about learning truly to listen to God? How can we learn to listen to God, and how can we help others do that? Here are a few thoughts:

(1) Samuel had people who cared about him. Especially his mother and father but also the priest Eli cared about him. Trusted people who love us are a great help in learning to listen to God ourselves and thus discovering what we are to do and the way we are to go.

(2) Samuel sought guidance from Eli. It's good that for all the faults of Eli he was able to give good guidance to Samuel about what to do about listening to God and telling God's message. It's good to have people to whom we can go for guidance as we seek to listen to God and find God's way for our lives.

How else can we recognize God's voice more clearly and respond?

(3) We should recognize that God often acts through the circumstances of our lives. That includes the needs that we see around us, the opportunities that we have, and the abilities or gifts that we recognize in ourselves, often with the help of others. Back to Steven Spielberg. He tells how he got started in filmmaking as a child through a project for a Boy Scout merit badge. When the audience of his fellow children howled with laughter at his film, he was hooked for life.[11] So what needs do you see, what gifts do you have, and what are the opportunities of your life?

(4) We should measure all that we find and hear by what Scriptures tells about Jesus. People sometimes do crazy and even destructive things because they insist that God told them to do them, but they never listened to and learned from Jesus.

(5) We should be ready and willing to act on what we sense God is asking. As the old hymn states, "Lord, Speak to Me That I May Speak."[12]

(6) We would do well not to insist on knowing all the details before we say *yes*. If we knew all

the details, we'd probably say *no*. Would Samuel have said *yes* to God's call if he had known all the hard things he was going to have to do and go through, not just at the beginning but all through his life? Maybe Samuel would, but will we? Samuel made at least one bad decision, and he made decisions that were good but that everybody didn't like. He paid a price in both situations.

(7) In seeking to listen to God, we would be helped by recognizing that God generally whispers rather than shouts. So, let us listen for God's whispers, and let us be willing to act in faith without being completely certain.

4.

Mark 2:13-22
Follow the Leader

Eighth Sunday after the Epiphany

"Follow me." That was Jesus' invitation—or was it a command?—to Levi in our text.

Imagine Levi telling his story about what happened to him that day. Perhaps it would go something like this:

> I looked up—and there he was. . . . I stared at him, and he stared at me. . . . I started shuffling my feet. And he smiled. You know the way he smiles sometimes all of a sudden—and he says, "Follow me." I couldn't believe my ears. I tumbled out of my desk, and away he went up the street, and I went after him. I could hear people laughing—and somebody spat at me—but I didn't seem to care.[13]

> I was so happy. He accepted me just like he accepted everybody else—me, a tax collector! It didn't seem to matter to him that lots of people hated me for what I did. He loved me. *He* loved *me!* I could hardly believe it, but I knew it was true.

I thought of my friends who were just like me. I wanted them to know him, too. So I gave a dinner party at my house and invited them all. When they got there and found Jesus there, too, you should have seen the looks on their faces! They were *amazed*. Jesus came over to every one of them and said, "Hello, I'm Jesus. I'm so glad to finally meet you. I want you to follow me."

Well, maybe that's the way it happened. Whatever the case, those words capture for me some of the excitement, freedom, and joy of life in Christ. This life is concerned first of all for Christ himself and cares little about what other people may think.

Within this experience of Jesus' call of Levi and then the dinner party with the other tax collectors that followed, I want you to see the two steps every person needs to take if we are to follow Jesus, our leader. We need to take these two steps if we would have in our lives the excitement, freedom, joy, and love that Levi seems to have had, and if we would mean the most in the service of Christ.

Conversion

The first step is the step of conversion. Jesus said to Levi, "Follow me" (Mark 2:14). And Levi rose and followed him. Then—and only then—did the new life in Christ begin for him. I'd like to lead you to consider several things about Levi's conversion, conversion in general, and your conversion in particular.

First—conversion is a necessity. Jesus didn't come preaching that perhaps it would be a good idea sometime, when you get around to it, to ponder how things might be a little better if you would think about making whatever minor adjustment in your life that would help you feel better about God and maybe even yourself and others. Hardly! Jesus came saying, "The time is fulfilled, and the kingdom of God has come near; repent, and believe in the good news" (1:15). Jesus' message began with a statement and ended with a command. "Repent and believe in the good news." To do that was a necessity, a must. It's not *perhaps*, it's not a minor concern, it's not a suggestion, but rather it's a necessity.

That's the way it was with Levi. That's the way it is with us. There is no self-help plan, no list of ten suggestions, that will do the job. We need to be converted.

Conversion is a necessity. Levi knew this. Tax collectors could make a comfortable living. They had steady jobs. But Levi somehow must have known he needed more than this. So he listened to Jesus intently and responded eagerly.

Do we know that conversion is a necessity? These days the idea of conversion seems a bit antiquated, something that can be relegated to the crusades and revival meetings of former years. I wouldn't be surprised if some folks cringe when they read or hear that word. But conversion is a necessity. Quite often we are satisfied if people we know and love can get good jobs, live in good houses, be decent and respectable, and not bother anyone or be bothered by anyone. All of that would be good, of course. But could there be more? Jesus came to show us that there is indeed more and to make it available to us.

There are those words of Jesus. "Repent, and believe in the good news" (1:15). "Follow me" (2:14). Conversion is a necessity.

A second thing Levi's conversion teaches is that *conversion is not just a necessity but a possibility.* Levi and his tax collector friends might well have known deep down in their hearts that conversion was a necessity. What they might have doubted was whether conversion was a possibility *for them.* The whole thrust of the religion of their day was that a right relationship with God was not possible for people like them. They were on the wrong side of the fence from God, according to the people who built the fences. They couldn't meet the standards set up by the religious leaders. They were untouchables; they couldn't get to God. Would God accept people like them? Of course not.

Then Jesus came. Unlike the Pharisees, who kept their distance from such people, Jesus sought out Levi. Not only that, Jesus told Levi, "Follow me." And that's what Levi did.

Then Levi gave a dinner part to introduce his friends in low places to Jesus. The Pharisees showed up, too, since given the nature of the housing of that day, even private dinner parties could be rather public.

At the dinner party, the Pharisees challenged Jesus about the people with whom he associated. Jesus explained that well people don't need a doctor, but sick people do. He had come to help the sick people.

I doubt that Jesus was saying that the Pharisees were well and didn't need him. No, the Pharisees simply didn't know that they were sick, with the "sickness unto death" of which Kierkegaard spoke centuries later. They were sick. But they were not willing to hear the diagnosis or receive the miracle cure that was available.

Jesus came saying that conversion was indeed possible for Levi and for all those like him. It is possible for you, too. Maybe you've been down so far at some time or other that you questioned whether conversion was possible. Maybe you're that way today. Maybe you've been involved in some things that you think were pretty bad and even unforgivable.

I've got good news. Conversion is a possibility for you, even you, even me.

Note a third teaching about conversion. *Conversion is life-changing.* Conversion makes a difference in your life when it's real. Levi heard Jesus' invitation, "Follow me." Levi responded, and the whole experience changed his life forever.

Conversion makes a difference, a life-changing difference. As I heard a teenager testify once, conversion enables you to get your life together and to start doing what you need to do with it.

Conversion makes a life-changing difference. It doesn't make you perfect, and it doesn't take away all your problems. After conversion, you will still not be perfect and will still have problems. But conversion does start a person walking in the right direction on the right road toward the right goal. It puts you in touch with the strength to make the journey, and it helps you deal with the problems you face. Conversion makes a life-changing difference.

Think about your conversion for a moment if you have experienced conversion. Some people talk about *the plan of salvation* as if there were just one—*the* plan. In a way, there is, basically. It's *ABC*—accept your need of Christ; believe that God has sent Christ to provide your need; commit your life to Christ. But the New Testament seems to indicate that God tailor-makes the conversion experience for each one of us, according to our own backgrounds and needs. Levi's experience wasn't like Paul's, you know. People who give every evidence of being Christians have described their conversion experiences in one of five basic ways:

First, unconscious conversion. People who had an unconscious conversion had no awareness of a point in time at which they became Christians. Yet all the normal ways by which Christians can be identified applied to them.

Second, gradual conversion. People who described their conversion experience as gradual indicated that it seemed to them to have taken place over a period of time rather than in one blinding flash.

Third, conversion by steps. People could identify a number of experiences in their lives that in themselves did not fully satisfy their quest until a final confirming experience occurred.

Fourth, sudden conversion. People who experienced what they identified as "sudden conversion" had an experience like Paul's. They likely did not see a blinding light, but they can point to a single, dramatic, emotional experience to describe their conversion.

Fifth, conversion and reconversion. People who understood their salvation experience in this manner believe they made a good decision early in life but then found the need to update it later, probably as adults. Sometimes this "reconversion" is expressed as a "rededication," a "call to the ministry," or a "call to mission service."

Which one best describes your experience? A Damascus road experience like Paul's is generally held up as the norm, but one survey shows that most people identified more with the gradual awakening rather than a single event.[14]

You may have a different opinion, but I don't think it matters much the exact nature of your conversion experience. What matters is that you have indeed met Christ and given your life to him. What matters, too, is how this affects your life now.

There's one other thing you need to see about conversion. Conversion is the beginning and not the final step in the Christian life. Someone has pointed out that conversion is indeed the end of salvation, but it's the front end. Conversion is the beginning of the Christian life. Levi had a lot of following Jesus to do after he first rose and followed him.

I encourage you to ask yourself about your conversion, about whether you have truly given your life to Jesus. Have you taken this first step in following Jesus? You ought to ask, too, whether you have followed Jesus anywhere after you rose and followed him that first time. That brings us to the second step in this two-step movement of following Jesus.

Concern

The second step is the step Levi took in giving the dinner party. It's the step of concern. Concern for other people is an integral part of being converted. It's not the way you get converted, but it's a step within conversion that shows the reality of your conversion or at least your obedience to Jesus.

Some people say they come to church to get their batteries charged. A wise person asked, "What for?" The answer is right here in the second step. The "what-for" is concern for people.

We see this concern so vividly in Jesus, especially here in this section of Scripture. Mark 2:1 to 3:6 forms something of a unit in Mark's Gospel. There are five questions about Jesus' authority in this unit. All of them have to do also with Jesus' concern for people.

The first question is in Mark 2:7—"Who can forgive sins but God alone?" Jesus had just said to a paralyzed person, "Your sins are forgiven" (2:5). Jesus had shown his concern for people in this act of forgiveness.

The second occurs in this very passage that is our text. Jesus was eating with the lowlifes of that society. The Pharisees asked, "Why does he eat with tax collectors and sinners?" (2:17). Because they needed help, that's why, as Jesus would tell them in that very verse.

The third question comes when the Pharisees want to know why Jesus' disciples didn't fast like they and John's disciples did (2:18). Jesus replied that it was a time for joy, not fasting. The presence of the kingdom meant joy for people.

The fourth and fifth questions were about keeping the rules about the Sabbath. In both instances, Jesus replied that human need took precedence over the customs and rules of people, even religious people.

So these questions and their responses show us clearly that Jesus was concerned about people. Have we taken this second step with him?

This is serious, important business these days. When a friend of mine was pastor of a huge church in a metropolitan area, he and the church wanted to find ways to reach the people of the area and find out what barriers they had to cross to do that. So they hired a marketing firm to find out what people thought about their denomination and mine—Baptists. Uh-oh, right? Those interviewed were asked to rank Baptists, Catholics, Methodists, Pentecostals, and the Church of Christ on identification by certain words. Baptists ranked first in words such as "pushy," "self-serving," "cliquish," "discriminates," "fundamentalist," and "hateful." They ranked next to last in descriptions such as "loving," "diversified," "open-minded," and "modern."

Actually, these results are no surprise to me and probably not to you considering the people who are getting air time on national television and calling themselves Baptists. I'm getting weary of saying that I'm not that kind of Baptist—but I'm not, at least I try not to be.

Frankly, Christians have got a lot of negative PR to overcome. But we can do it if we deepen and broaden our concern for one another and indeed, for all people. What keeps us from genuine concern? Several things, I'm sure.

One is defensiveness. Sometimes we are afraid to reach out to other people, or even to one another, because we want to protect what we have. We fail to see, though, that what we have and are, we have and are by God's grace. Moreover, God's grace is sufficient for our every need, even if we must lose what we think we must protect right now. If God loves us by grace, then we must communicate to others that God so loves them, too.

Furthermore, we must communicate this to *all* other people, not just to people of our ethnicity, social class, or other human category. The Pharisees had not done this. Their defensiveness blocked their concern for other people. They might well have had great fellowship with their fellow Pharisees, but they were judgmental and discriminatory toward other people, especially Levi's kind of people.

A second barrier to genuine concern is an inordinate emphasis on rule-keeping. Mainly by this we mean keeping the rules we ourselves think are important. Rule-keeping is a way of controlling life and controlling and other people. It's pretty judgmental, isn't it?

Prejudice is a third blockade to deepening and broadening our concern for others. This problem occurs when we judge people on the basis of external factors—their looks, for example.

A friend of mine who is pastor of First Baptist Church, Amarillo, Texas, tells a great story.[15] It didn't happen in his church but in a church somewhere else. It's a true story, even if it didn't happen, and who knows for sure whether it did. It's the story of Bill.

Bill was a college student. His whole wardrobe consisted of well-worn jeans and T-shirts with holes. He was very bright. Somehow, somewhere, he accepted Christ as Savior. He decided to come to church. So he did. He got there late, looked for a seat, and couldn't find one. The church was packed. Bill kept moving toward the front. He finally wound up at the very front. Then he realized there were no seats, and so he simply sat down on the carpet. No one had ever done that before in that church. The pastor was watching all of this from his place on the stage.

Then the pastor and the congregation saw an elderly deacon making his way from the back of the church. There couldn't be a bigger contrast between this elderly deacon and this wildly-dressed young man. The elderly deacon had on a nice suit, a white shirt, and a tie. If you had looked up *dignified* in the dictionary, you would have seen his picture. If you had looked up *weird* in the dictionary, you would have seen Bill's. The elderly deacon walked with a cane.

You could almost hear some in the congregation saying to themselves, "You can't blame him for what we know he's going to do. He's going to ask the kid to leave. How can you expect someone his age and background to understand and appreciate some shabbily-dressed college kid sitting on the floor?"

The elderly deacon finally reached the young man. All eyes were on the two of them. The preacher might as well have stopped preaching; no one was paying attention. Then the elderly man dropped his cane on the floor and, with great difficulty, he lowered himself and sat down next to Bill. It was so natural it was like he did that every Sunday.

Do I have to tell you that everyone in the congregation had a lump in their throat that day? It might have been a two-lump day, in fact. Everybody learned about that second step of following Jesus—concern.

What if someone like Bill came to your church and did that? Do you know what would happen? Would there be one person or maybe a half-dozen all ages sitting down there on the floor with him? Would you love people with the love of Christ?

You don't have to tell me that that's not easy to do, certainly not all of the time. Still, though, we must find ways to overcome our ideas about each other and other people even though sometimes that's not easy.

So we must take this step of concern for other people within our fellowship—and beyond it. How sobering and challenging it is to realize that unless someone out there can come to trust you and feel your concern for them that they may never come to trust God and feel God's concern for them. If you claim to be a Christian, some people blame God for what they see in you or fail to see in you. If they see in you lovelessness, coldness, judgmentalism, and unconcern, they feel that God himself is like this. They are driven away and not drawn closer to him.

Whatever mistakes we make in our churches and that we make in our individual lives, let us not make the mistake of failing to let people know that we love them. If people cannot feel love from you whom they have seen, how can we expect them to feel love from God whom they have not seen?

Church is for the people who've been ground down, left out, put down, and passed over. We're here to help them get included in, put back together, and lifted up.

So, have you trusted Christ and been converted? And, have you followed Christ into a life of concern for people? Today is the day to follow the leader—truly *the* Leader, Jesus.

5.

John 3:14-21
Your Spiritual Survival Kit

Fourth Sunday in Lent

I'm sure you know what a survival kit is. In the military, such a kit contains the basics of what is needed to survive if you find yourself in the wilderness.

This text provides something similar and a great deal more. It's a spiritual survival kit, but more, it's a spiritual victory kit. For, as 1 John 4:4 states, "the one who is in you is greater than the one who is in the world." Too, as Paul states, "Thanks be to God, who in Christ always leads us in triumphal procession" (2 Corinthians 2:14).

This spiritual survival kit or spiritual victory kit can be seen in one verse in this text. That verse, as you might guess, is John 3:16, "For God so loved the world that he gave his only Son, so that everyone who believes in him may not perish but may have eternal life." This verse suggests three items for the spiritual victory kit.

The Love God Sends

If you forget everything else, remember this: God loves you. People have many different ideas about

God and what God is like. But over and over, Scripture affirms this truth: God loves you. And it's a wonderful truth. And so is what it means in life. Love "bears all things, believes all things, hopes all things, endures all things" (1 Corinthians 13:7). This is true of love between people, but it is especially true of God's love.

How do we know God loves us? We could name many things, but the main thing is found in John 3:16. God "gave his only Son." God did not have to do this. God could have ignored us, but God sent his Son.

In Jesus, and especially in Jesus' death on the cross, we see unmistakably that God loves us. As Jesus himself said, "No one has greater love than this, to lay down one's life for one's friends" (John 15:13). God loves us.

What does this love do for us? God's love provides the way of salvation. "For the wages of sin is death, but the free gift of God is eternal life in Christ Jesus our Lord" (Romans 6:23).

Too God's love provides strength for living. "The Spirit helps us in our weakness; for we do not know how to pray as we ought, but that very Spirit intercedes with sighs too deep for words" (Rom. 8:26).

Moreover, God's love provides final victory over our greatest enemy and fear, death. Jesus, the epitome of God's love, said, "I am the resurrection and the life. Those who believe in me, even though they die, will live, and everyone who lives and believes in me will never die" (John 11:25-26).

The Faith You Live

God sent his Son so that "everyone who believes in him may not perish but may have eternal life" (3:16). "Everyone who believes in him," the text says. "This is the victory that conquers the world, our faith," 1 John 5:4 states.

There may be times when our faith is weak. There may even be times when we feel we've lost or almost lost faith. But hang onto whatever smidgen of faith you can. Even when your faith is just a glimmer, smaller than a mustard seed, you will find it is enough. Even a small amount of faith is worthwhile.

Faith is not just something you have, too. Faith is something you live. In the Greek, the word translated *faith* is not a noun, but a verb. Too, our English word *belief* comes from the expression *by life*. That means that genuine faith is active in life, not just in our minds.

Genuine faith ought to make a difference in how we live. So the faith we live goes in our spiritual survival kit along with God's love.

The Promise God Keeps

The rest of John 3:16 emphasizes the promise God keeps—"may not perish but may have eternal life." As is often true of the words the Gospel of John uses, the word translated "eternal" has more than one meaning.

The word means "eternal" in quantity. How long will you have life, the life the God of love gives through his Son? Forever. That is what God promises.

"Eternal life" also refers to an unmatched quality of life. In the Gospel of John, "eternal life" means knowing God—truly, intimately knowing God. That means living the best kind of life. That means abundant life. There may well be difficulties, problems, and unhappiness, of course, for many reasons. But through it all, we are not alone; God is with us. And we have God's power to help us.

Jesus said, "My sheep hear my voice. I know them, and they follow me. I give them eternal life, and they will never perish. No one will snatch them out of my hand. What my Father has given me is greater than all else, and no one can snatch it out of the Father's hand" (11:27-30).

These few things go in your spiritual survival kit—the love God sends, the faith you live, the promise of eternal life that we can trust God to keep. You will find they are enough for whatever you need to face, now and forever.[16]

6.

Mark 14:3-9, 22-25, 32-36
Some Things Can't Wait

Liturgy of the Passion: Sixth Sunday in Lent

Some things can't wait. The Gospel of Mark gives that distinct impression, for sure. Throughout all of Mark's Gospel, one Greek word is used over and over again. Depending on the English translation, the word is translated "immediately" or "at once."

After Jesus' baptism by John, "the Spirit immediately drove him out into the wilderness" (Mark 1:12). After Jesus had taught and healed in the synagogue at Capernaum, "at once his fame began to spread . . ." (1:28). "Immediately" after Jesus' stilling of the storm, Jesus "spoke to them and said, 'Take heart, it is I; do not be afraid'" (6:51). And there are many other such time references in the Gospel of Mark. It is as if Mark breathlessly tells the gospel story because there is no time to waste.

Some things can't wait. For Mark, telling Jesus' story was one of those *can't wait* actions.

Some people, and maybe all of us sometime, evidently think there is plenty of time to waste. True, some of us need to learn not to be so driven by clocks and calendars. But it's still true also that some things can't wait.

Maybe you know of a person whom you could swear must have been born a half-hour late and they've been late ever since. (If you are always or almost always the last one to arrive, no matter what the occasion, maybe *you* are that person.) If your outlook is such that you think there is plenty of time to waste, think about the other side for a few moments.

Shakespeare said it:

> There is a tide in the affairs of men
> [and women],
> Which, taken at the flood, leads on to
> fortune;
> Omitted all the voyages of their life
> Is bound in shallows and in miseries;
> And we must take the current when it
> serves,
> Or lose our ventures.[17]

The bard was saying in poetic language that some things can't wait.

In his autobiography, Billy Graham tells of a university student who asked him what was the greatest surprise he had found about life. Graham replied without hesitation, "The brevity of it."[18] When my daddy was in his seventies, he told me something similar. He said, "Son, you're going to be surprised at how quick it passes." The "it" in that sentence refers to life. I've found that he was completely accurate. Life passes quickly. Some things can't wait, and life is one of them.

Mark 14 is filled with events that just couldn't wait. Three incidents stand out.

Risky Giving

The incident in Mark 14:3-9 happened at the home of Simon the leper, which was at Bethany near Jerusalem. The occasion was a dinner party, a very happy time.

Few knew, however, that the party was the calm before the storm that was about to erupt. Only Jesus, in fact, knew what lay ahead.

It was the last week of Jesus' life. Already detailed plans were underway to arrest Jesus and kill him. The religious leaders who opposed Jesus had been planning to destroy him for some time. Mark 3:6 has this comment after an incident early in Jesus' ministry: "The Pharisees went out and immediately conspired with the Herodians against him, how to destroy him." Now, more than ever, they wanted to *get him.* They hoped only for a quiet moment away from the crowds so they could arrest Jesus, get rid of him, and thus *be* rid of him once and for all.

But for now, at the home of Simon, things were quiet and peaceful, even joyful. Then something shocking happened.

A woman came with an alabaster jar of ointment, very expensive ointment. She is not identified further in the Gospel of Mark. The woman broke the jar and proceeded to anoint Jesus' head with the ointment.

What does the broken jar signify? It shows that she intended to use all of the ointment in anointing Jesus. She was not saving some back for another time. The time was now.

The ointment was very expensive. Very likely the ointment cost more, much more, than a tenth of her income; this was an extravagance (see the similar incident in John 12:5). But the time to do it was now.

All were not pleased with what the woman did. Everybody never is. The woman's action made some—evidently some of the followers of Jesus—indignant. They became huffy. Really, they were angry. What a waste, they thought. It could have been used much more practically. It could have been given to the poor, for example.

Jesus' reaction was different, though. Of course, Jesus cared for the poor, too. Hadn't he fed thousands of hungry people in his lifetime? But Jesus' reaction to the woman's extravagant act was utterly unexpected. He called what the woman did "a good service" to him. Literally he called it *a beautiful act*. The woman's act was not just good; it was gracious, lovely, beautiful.

Jesus went on to explain that this was the opportune time to help him. The time was now. Her anointing of him was actually in preparation beforehand for his burial. The woman's lavish, extravagant act was altogether kind and loving, for it was preparation for what Jesus had to face.

Jesus appreciated tremendously her loving deed. She had done it, and she had done it at decidedly the right time. The woman was to be remembered everywhere the gospel was preached, the whole world around, as long as time itself, for her lavish, generous, beautiful act.

The woman is a beautiful example of risky living and truly generous giving. She did what she was able to do. Like the poor widow who gave all her resources for living, this woman who anointed Jesus gave extravagantly, lavishly, in a risky manner (see Mark 12:41-44). And there was no time to do it like the time in which she did it. If she had waited another week to do what she did, she would have missed forever the opportunity.

She is an example for our own living and giving, too. She did not measure out her life with a medicine-dropper. Rather, she gave abundantly. And she gave at the most appropriate time, when it mattered the most—now.

Why did she do it? Like the rude people who complained about her, are we really able to fathom it either? Why couldn't she have been more practical? Why didn't she just give half, say, to Jesus, save a fourth for a rainy day, and use another fourth for this person or that cause, perhaps even giving it to the poor? Wouldn't that have been more practical? Why didn't she cut her gift in pieces and carefully parcel it out?

Here's a likely answer. The woman had her priorities in life set. Nothing and no one was more important to her than Jesus. Her love for Jesus led her to commit herself and what she had to Jesus and Jesus alone. So she simply gave it all to Jesus. She was boldly extravagant instead of calculating.

What a beautiful picture of life she presents. Her attitude of risky giving lifted what we might consider as mere duty to beauty. She gave excessively and lavishly and left for us a learning that is indispensable for abundant living.

Likely we have all felt tugged this way and that for our time, our energy, and our money. When we feel tugged like that, often the reason is that the priorities of our lives are not set properly. We are still parceling out our lives in little pieces, and we are afraid there is not enough to go around. As a result, we find ourselves living considerably less than abundantly. Why? Because we are not giving bountifully to the one who demands our full allegiance, Jesus.

For most of her life, a woman named Gert Behanna went from husband to husband, bottle to bottle, and from suicide attempt to suicide attempt. As she gave her testimony across the nation at numerous church gatherings, she told how she had been living anything but abundantly, even though she had a vast fortune. Something happened to her, though. She met Jesus as her Savior. She began to give bountifully of herself and her fortune. She even gave away her fortune, saying, "Money is like bricks: you can slug people with them or use them to build . . . ." She almost waited too late to learn that truth, but she learned it just in time and made a world of difference to many people.

Is this risky? You bet. But remember,

> Jesus didn't say, "Come follow me, and I will make you . . . feel good."

Jesus didn't say, "Come follow me, and I will make you . . . rich."

Jesus didn't say, "Come follow me, and I will make you . . . successful."

Jesus did say, "Come follow me, and I will make you fishers of men and women."

Jesus did say, "Come follow me, . . . take up your cross."[19]

Some things just can't wait.

Meaningful Giving

Look at a second incident in this chapter in verses 22-25. This incident draws a picture of meaningful giving. We see this picture in Jesus' Last Supper with his disciples.

The disciples were gathered for what they thought was merely a celebration of the Passover. A surprise lay ahead. At the appropriate time in the meal, Jesus took the bread, blessed it, broke it, and gave it to the disciples. "Take, this is my body," he said (Mark 14:22). Then Jesus took the cup, gave thanks, and gave it to them, and they all drank of it.

Was Jesus merely giving them bread and drink? Of course not. He was giving them himself in a meaningful way as he gave them the bread and the cup. In giving the disciples the bread, Jesus was giving them himself in sacrifice for them and in an eternal fellowship with them. He would give his very body in sacrifice for them. They would be reminded every time they broke bread that Jesus was forever with them. In giving the disciples the cup, Jesus was giving them himself, his own life-blood, and thereby sealing God's new covenant with people through his sacrificial death.

Jesus' giving of the bread and the cup was meaningful giving. We may need to learn more about this sort of giving, for much of our giving may not be as meaningful as it could be.

Some giving that we do we do out of necessity, even compulsion. We give a few dollars or write a check because we would be embarrassed for others to know we hadn't. Our heart is really not in it. We know it, the Lord knows it, and in some cases others know it even though we have tried hard not to let them know. It's giving, and that's good as far as it goes, but it's not exactly heartfelt. If that's as good as you can do right now, don't stop. You may well get better at it as time goes along.

On the other hand, sometimes by the grace of God we give meaningfully. Our money is representative of our love and concern. We earnestly desire that the gospel be preached and that people be helped. We give our time because we care for and believe in something very strongly. We really give ourselves, not just to get someone off our backs, but because we care. We give in such a way that our money and our time are truly representative of our body given and our blood poured out.

Such giving is meaningful giving. The object to which we give our time, energy, and money has our hearts.

We ought not be satisfied with our giving of mere money until it is like that—truly meaningful, involving *us*. Such giving is not a substitute for ourselves but truly represents ourselves. How much will you need to give for your giving to be meaningful?

Sacrificial Giving

A third picture in this chapter teaches about the depth of giving, and this picture appears in verses 32-36. This picture is of the kind of giving that just can't wait.

We get this picture from a man prostrate on the ground in urgent, agonizing prayer. If we would go closer and could stay awake long enough, we would hear him saying something like this: *Daddy, Father, you can do all things. Take this terrible cup away from me. Do not let me have to face the horror of the cross. Spare me this. But I yield myself to your will completely. Not what I want but what you want be done.* In this urgent prayer, Jesus left us an unsurpassed example of sacrificial giving.

Is sacrificial giving demanded of us, too? That question can be answered by a second question. Did Jesus say, "Follow me"?

When we hear talk about sacrificial giving, our impulse is to explain why this really doesn't apply to us. We say knowingly to one another, *I don't believe Jesus really meant such and such, do you?*

Does Jesus really demand sacrificial giving? What if we just give *as much as we can?* So how close to sacrifice would that really be? That generally translates into *what's left after we've gotten all of the things we need and most of the things we want.* Is that sacrificial giving?

Some things can't wait. Deciding to give bountifully, meaningfully, and sacrificially is one of them. Only as we recognize that and give accordingly will we make the difference we need to make. Some things do get too late, and opportunities are missed.

A missionary tells the true story of watching a businessperson open his cash register. The missionary was surprised to see among the bills and coins a six-inch nail. The missionary asked, "What's that nail for?" The businessperson replied, "I keep this nail with my money to remind me of the price that Christ paid for my salvation and of what I owe him in return." Some things can't wait.

That is so for people of every age. If you're in your senior adult years, you know very well that some things just can't wait. But that is so if you're in your middle years or if you're a young adult.

When my first book came out a few years ago, I did interview after interview with the news media, almost 100 of them in a six-month stretch, including CNN. I did book promotion tours to a number of cities across the United States. One of the highlights was a booksigning at the American Booksellers Association in New York. In a thirty-minute period, I signed dozens of books. Next to me, though, was a real celebrity—Erma Bombeck. She had had a weekly newspaper column for many years, she had published many books, and she was a regular on *Good Morning America*. I'm sure she signed hundreds and hundreds of books. The line for her table stretched all around the huge room we were in.

When the booksigning was over, she and I were left pretty much alone in this large room. Unlike some celebrities, she had no entourage, and she didn't rush off. In fact, she came over to me, gracious lady that she was, and she engaged me in a few moments of chit-chat about the booksigning. We walked out together. She was warm, genuine, gracious, and attractive.

As you may recall, she died of cancer some years ago. She was often asked how she gathered ideas for columns. Did she save up ideas for the future? One of her final columns spoke to this. The column was titled, "What's Saved Is Often Lost." This is what she wrote:

> I don't save anything. My pockets are empty at the end of a week. So is my gas tank. So is my file of ideas. I trot out the best I've got, and come the next week, I bargain, whimper, make promises, cower and throw myself on the mercy of the Almighty for just three more columns in exchange for cleaning my oven . . . .
>
> Throughout the years, I've seen a fair number of my family who have died leaving candles that have never been lit, appliances that never got out of the box . . . .

I have learned that silver tarnishes when it isn't used, . . . candles melt in the attic over the summer, and ideas that are saved for a dry week often become dated.

I always had a dream that when I am asked to give an accounting of my life to a higher court, it will be like this: "So, empty your pockets. What have you got left of your life? Any dreams that were unfilled? Any unused talent that we gave you when you were born that you still have left? Any unsaid compliments or bits of love that you haven't spread around?"

And I will answer, "I've nothing to return. I spent everything you gave me. I'm as naked as the day I was born."[20]

Yes, what's saved up is often lost, and so is what is put off. Some things can't wait.

7.
John 13:1-17, 31b-35
What Life Is Meant to Be Like
Maundy Thursday

What is life meant to be like? In a real sense Jesus addressed that question in what he did here at the Last Supper.

The end of Jesus' life on earth was quickly approaching. Only a few hours remained before he would be taken violently, tried unjustly, and crucified unmercifully. He seems to have sought to make the most of the brief moments of his life that remained.

How challenging it is to us to see what Jesus chose to do in that pressure-filled time, especially here at the Last Supper with his disciples. How instructive it is to us to see what Jesus tried to teach his disciples about himself and how life is to be lived. Jesus used a vivid, heart-touching object lesson to teach them and us what life is meant to be like.

This lesson from Jesus became indelibly imprinted on the minds and hearts of the disciples. They certainly did not practice it perfectly from that point on, but they could never forget it. It was that vivid. What Jesus did in washing the disciples' feet showed unmistakably what his own life was like and what life—yours, mine—is meant to be like. As we look at this lesson in this passage, we see several elements in the picture of what was occurring that day.

Jesus as Servant

First, when we see Jesus acting as and, indeed, *being* a servant, we see the importance of servanthood, of acting as and *being* servants ourselves. Jesus was always doing the unexpected, catching people off-guard, wasn't he? He ate meals with outcasts; he engaged a woman—a *Samaritan* woman at that—in conversation; he hugged little children when other people thought he had better things to do.

Get the picture of what was happening in this passage. Here was Jesus, the renowned miracle-worker, healer, and teacher. Crowds had flocked to him in the past, for they recognized in him something special. Indeed, they saw that Jesus himself was *someone* special. Moreover, Jesus was the one whom the disciples had confessed to be the Christ, the Son of God. They called him "Teacher" and "Lord."

This was the last night of Jesus' earthly life, and he knew it. Given who Jesus was, did he take a purple robe and place it around himself? Did he take a crown covered with costly jewels and place it on his head? Did he take in his hand a golden scepter, fit for the King of kings? Did he sit on a throne and call his disciples to bow before him and worship him? No, none of that. He could have, I suppose, but he didn't.

What did Jesus do? He rose from supper, laid aside his outer garments, girded himself with a towel, poured water into a basin, and—unbelievably—began to wash the dusty, dirty feet of his disciples. He even wiped them with a towel. He was doing what only slaves or Gentile servants would do. Given this, of all that Jesus had done, perhaps this act was the most unbelievable and beyond all expectations.

Someone has said that if you want to see what a person is like, give that person power. Jesus had been given all power, all authority, in heaven and on earth. Look what Jesus did with it.

Jesus used this power for others, not himself. In humility, he became a servant. He washed and wiped the disciples' dirty feet. Do you want to get a clearer picture of those feet? Have you ever spent any time in a barnyard, where cows, horses, and chickens walk and live? That's what the streets of Jerusalem and the other first-century towns were like. Think again about those dirty feet that had walked in those streets. Picture Jesus washing them, and you will have an unforgettable picture.

This unforgettable picture shows us the importance of being a servant. That was really Jesus' role—a servant, indeed, *the* servant. Jesus' work was to aid, to comfort, to give. He "emptied himself, taking the form of a slave," Paul said (Philippians 2:7). Jesus came to earth, associated with common folks as one of them and even lower than them, for he washed their feet. He died on a cross as a common criminal. As Jesus himself put it, "For the Son of Man came not to be served but to serve, and to give his life a ransom for many" (Mark 10:45).

This picture of Jesus as Servant shows us the importance of servanthood as we seek to picture what life is meant to be like. A second part of the picture is

Humanity as It Really Is

Peter represents us, all of us, as Jesus sought to wash his feet. Peter was perplexed, puzzled. He asked, "Lord, are you going to wash my feet?" (John 13:6). This was not Peter's idea of what Messiah was to do and be. Peter would much prefer the Messiah sitting on a throne rather than washing his feet. We have seen this in Peter before in the Gospels, for he had tried to persuade Jesus not to go to the cross and to convince Jesus that the cross was not his destiny.

Peter could not accept Jesus as a servant. Do you know why? I think it was because Peter was smart enough to follow the logic of it all. If Jesus was a servant, then Jesus' followers must be servants, too. Peter did not want this—not for Jesus and not for himself. Likely we have a hard time with this idea, too.

Jesus explained to Peter, "You do not know now what I am doing, but later you will understand" (13:7). Later? Jesus meant later, after the crucifixion, as Jesus gave his life, and after the resurrection, as Jesus' way of life was vindicated, affirmed, and approved as what life is meant to be like.

Peter still did not understand, but his puzzlement turned into pride. He insisted, "You will never wash my feet" (13:8). Servanthood would not be Peter's way, and it should not be Jesus' way. That is not really what life is meant to be like, is it?

But it is. Jesus was saying that servanthood is his way. Furthermore, if Peter did not accept that for Jesus and for himself, then Peter had not really gotten the message about who Jesus was. Jesus bluntly said, "Unless I wash you, you have no share with me" (13:8).

Jesus' statement reminds us that self-surrender is the first demand of discipleship. We are to live Jesus' way, not ours. Peter saw at least a part of this truth, for he said with exuberance, in essence, *If that's the way it is, if it's that necessary, then wash my hands and my head as well as my feet.*

Then Jesus taught a significant lesson. This lesson is the reason we can never rest on our laurels, smugly assuming we have it made spiritually or in almost any other way.

In verse 10, Jesus replied to Peter, "One who has bathed does not need to wash, except for the feet, but is entirely clean." Jesus was saying that if one has had a bath before coming to supper, the only need is to wash one's feet to cleanse the travel grime from them. That's all that is needed, but that is certainly needed. "Bathed" seems to refer to the conversion experience. Once done, it does not need to be repeated. But cleansing from the dust and dirt of one's daily travels, one's sins, is needed, and it is needed continually.

We need continually to be reminded that Jesus was a servant and that we ourselves are meant to be servants. That is what life is meant to be like.

Our Responsibilities

Consider now our own responsibilities. After Jesus had washed the feet of his disciples, had taken his garments again, and had resumed his place, he said (13:12-17),

> Do you know what I have done to you? You call me Teacher and Lord—and you are right, for that is what I am. So if I, your Lord and Teacher, have washed your feet, you also ought to wash one another's feet. For I have set you an example, that you also should do as I have done to you. Very truly, I tell you, servants are not greater than their master, nor are messengers greater than the one who sent them. If you know these things, you are blessed if you do them.

Note that Jesus asked, "Do you know what I have done to you?" (13:12). Jesus had shown the disciples not only who he was but also what their responsibilities were.

Jesus did this by giving them an unforgettable example. If Jesus, the Lord of glory, acted in this way, then they—and we—ought to be willing to be servants. If we claim to be servants of Jesus, we must be servants of one another.

Jesus' deed and his words show us what he expects of us. They show us what life is meant to be like. And, Jesus' deed and his words give us yet another part of the picture. They show us the true way to happiness in life.

The True Way to Happiness in Life

Jesus said, "If you know these things, you are blessed if you do them" (13:17). That word "blessed" translates the Greek word *makarios*. In shorthand, the word means *happy*. True happiness comes to the person who lives this way, as a servant, as Jesus lived. Being a servant brings happiness to ourselves, and it also brings happiness to others.

My wife was teaching a group of five-year-olds in church, and they were getting ready to paint. She got the shirts out and instructed the children to put them on backward, with the buttons in the back. She told them to help each other, and then it became clear this was not their first time to do this. She went to get other things ready for painting. She never dreamed what they would do. She looked around, and all the children were standing in a neat row. Each child was buttoning the shirt of the child directly in front.

Let us learn from these children. Being a servant brings happiness in life for others and for ourselves, too.

William Barclay, the British Bible scholar and popular commentator on the New Testament, wrote,

> The greatest [people] regarded as their greatest honour the fact that they were servants of God. There was no higher title to which they could aspire. The summit of their ambition was the service of God. . . . No [person] can be anything greater than the servant of God.[21]

The concluding verses of the text sum up Jesus' deed and words for us (13:34-35):

> I give you a new commandment, that you love one another. Just as I have loved you, you also should love one another. By this everyone will know that you are my disciples, if you have love for one another.

This is what life is meant to be like.

8.

Mark 16:1-8
The Reality of the Resurrection

Resurrection of the Lord: Easter Day

Jesus' resurrection is the central doctrine of our Christian faith. Indeed, when Paul was talking about the resurrection in 1 Corinthians 15, he insisted that Jesus' resurrection is crucial, vital, absolutely necessary to the Christian faith. What happened in the tomb of Joseph of Arimathea in Jerusalem 2000 years ago one early morning in the Spring matters today, and it matters greatly.

As we consider this old, old story, let us focus today on two things about Jesus' resurrection. First, was it real? Second, is it real for us?

Was Jesus' Resurrection Real?

There was skepticism about Jesus' resurrection from the beginning. The Gospel of Matthew records the plot of the chief priests to pay off the soldiers guarding the tomb so they would say, "His disciples came by night and stole him away while we were asleep" (Matthew 28:13). The Book of Acts tells how the philosophers in Athens responded. "When they heard of the resurrection of the dead, some scoffed" (Acts 17:32).

The battle has been fought especially hard in the last two centuries. The predominant scientific worldview since the nineteenth century has been that there are no miracles. So we live in a locked-in, closed system with no place for something like the resurrection or anything out of the ordinary. All is to be explained in terms of what can be seen and felt. If we have not seen or experienced it in a verifiable manner, it does not exist. That is the reasoning regarding the resurrection.

Interestingly and perhaps surprisingly, the world was not so different in this regard in Jesus' time. Many people of Jesus' day were not so gullible as to be easily convinced, even in the name of religion.

Even Jesus' disciples were not gullible. They, too, especially Thomas in the Gospel of John, had to be convinced of the reality of Jesus' resurrection. They knew Jesus had been nailed to the cross on Friday, that he had died on Friday, and that he had been buried on Friday. He was dead, and they would not be easily convinced otherwise, any more than we would be if we had gone through that same set of experiences.

What convinced them that Jesus had really been raised from the dead? What overwhelmed their knowledge of Jesus' death with the belief that Jesus was now alive? As we answer this question, we will also be finding those things that can convince us today of the reality of Jesus' resurrection. Let us consider and put together three layers of proof.

First, the tomb was empty. For the women followers of Jesus in all four Gospels, and for Peter in the Gospels of Luke and John, the empty tomb began the process by which they began to be led to believe in Jesus' resurrection. The Scriptures tell us that only the beloved disciple in the Gospel of John was fully convinced of Jesus' resurrection because of the empty tomb. This "other disciple, who reached the tomb first, also went in, and he saw and believed" (John 20:8).

So the fact of the empty tomb was significant in leading to belief in Jesus' resurrection. There was no body. Jesus was not there. In spite of elaborate precautions by the Romans and the religious leaders, there was no body. Even the Roman soldiers could not keep Jesus in the tomb.

The tomb was empty. So one disciple believed, and some likely began to think, *Could it be?*

The next layer of proof was the resurrection appearances. Scripture records at least eleven and perhaps twelve. The earliest record in Scripture, in 1 Corinthians 15, mentions six resurrection appearances—"to Cephas, then to the twelve. Then to more than five hundred brothers and sisters at one time. . . . Then he appeared to James, then to all the apostles. Last of all, as to one untimely born he appeared also to me," said Paul (1 Corinthians 15:5-8).

Everyone in Jerusalem did not see the risen Jesus. Those to whom Jesus appeared were people of faith, able to receive the risen Lord as one raised from the dead. Even so, could all who saw him have been wrong? Would no one have said, *No, it didn't happen. They're all mistaken?* Possibly, I suppose, but we have no record of such a statement. Their testimonies are hard to discount.

There's an old story about a habitual criminal on trial for theft. The judge said, *Four people saw you steal it.* The thief replied, *Sure, your honor, but I can bring forty people who will swear they did not see me take it.* The testimony of forty who were ignorant of what happened had no weight against the testimony of four who saw it.

A third layer of evidence for the reality of the resurrection may be the most important. That evidence is the experience of the living Christ by the disciples and the church then and now. Look at what happened.

Before Jesus' resurrection, Peter was so fearful that he denied Jesus three times. After Jesus' resurrection, we find Peter standing firm against the authorities and preaching boldly.

Before Jesus' resurrection, James, the Lord's brother, was a scoffer and an unbeliever. He and the rest of Jesus' family considered Jesus to be borderline crazy. After Jesus' resurrection, we find James to be the leader of the church at Jerusalem. Could a dead leader have brought about such a change? Possibly, but the odds are very much against it.

Look at the change in the church as a whole. The church began to reach out and grow. It spread all over the Mediterranean area. Neither religious obstacles nor imperial edicts could stop the witness and growth of the church. Persecution and even death could not stop it. Could a faith founded on a lie have inspired such devotion? In light of events like the tragic Jim Jones movement of religious fanaticism several decades ago, honesty compels us to say, *Possibly.* But honesty also impels us to say, *Not likely.*

That we ourselves are gathered in Christian worship instead of in a pagan temple—or even gathered at all—is a sign of the reality of Jesus' resurrection. That we meet the first day of the week is a sign of the reality of Jesus' resurrection. That our lives have been changed through the Christian faith is a further sign of the reality of Jesus' resurrection.

So there are these three layers of proof—the empty tomb, the appearances of the risen Jesus, and the experiences of the early disciples, the church, and of ourselves. Taken together, they help us see the reality of the resurrection.

Is Jesus' Resurrection Real for Us?

What does Jesus' resurrection mean to us? Is it a mere long-ago event? How real is it to us, 2,000 years later and thousands of miles removed from us?

The reality of the resurrection impinges on our own reality in at least three ways. First, it shows us that righteousness—good—is really more powerful than evil.

Think about those followers of Jesus—women and men—who had walked and talked with Jesus over a period of many months. They had had confidence in Jesus. They believed in the message Jesus spoke and lived. For them, Jesus' death was a tragedy. The manner of his death was, in fact, a public disgrace. He had been condemned as a criminal, sentenced to death by crucifixion, and shamed in public. For these women and men who had followed Jesus, their hopes were all gone, their dreams shattered.

If the story of Jesus had ended at the cross, then unrighteousness, tragedy, and evil would be seen to be the dominant powers of the universe. But the resurrection says, *Not so.*

The resurrection shows that righteousness is more powerful than evil. God in Christ won the battle at the cross, and the resurrection demonstrated that victory to the world. Death could not hold Jesus. Jesus' resurrection shows good to be stronger than evil, truth to be more powerful than falsehood, the love of God to be stronger than the hatred of people, and God's power to be stronger than Satan's. With Jesus' resurrection, we see the victory of God's saving purpose that took Jesus to the cross.

The resurrection is real to us in another way. The resurrection signified the defeat of death. Jesus did not simply survive death. Rather, Jesus overcame death and defeated death. Jesus' resurrection does not mean simply that a part of

Jesus lived on, but that Jesus was resurrected. His nail-scarred body was transformed into a glorious body. Jesus lived on in the fullness of his personality.

The resurrection means this for us as well—the defeat of death. Oh, if history continues, we will have to die. But Jesus' resurrection assures us of our own resurrection. As Paul said in Romans 6:5, "For if we have been united with him in a death like his, we will certainly be united with him in a resurrection like his." Because Jesus' resurrection meant the defeat of death, we can know that God is able also to raise us up to eternal life in the fullness of our personalities.

The exact dimensions and details of life beyond death are not available to us. The important truth here, though, is that death does not have the last word about us or our loved ones who find their hope in Christ.

Considered a third way Jesus' resurrection can be real to us. The resurrection truly becomes real to us when we know that the resurrection means that Christ's ministry is being continued.

What was it Pilate, Annas, Caiaphas, and the other religious leaders were trying to do as they crucified Jesus? They were trying desperately to stop the ministry of Jesus. Jesus' life and words challenged their way of doing things. He was a threat to them. So they killed him.

So it was all over? So Jesus' ministry was stopped? No!

The resurrection tells us that Jesus' ministry goes on. It now is broadened to all the world and made more powerful as the risen Christ continues to minister and wishes to continue to minister through us.

Hear that again: Jesus' ministry continues through us. Because we are members of Christ's body, Jesus wishes to continue through us the ministry he began in Galilee and that the Romans and the religious leaders thought they had stopped when they crucified him. May God help us to experience and express the reality of Jesus' resurrection in our lives as we allow Jesus to continue his ministry through us.[22]

9.

1 John 1:1—2:2
What Is Christianity?
Second Sunday of Easter

What is Christianity? These verses from 1 John move us to ask this key question, a question we as Christians need to be prepared to answer. The marketing people challenge clients to give their *elevator speech* about their business or product. It's the speech that summarizes in a short elevator ride what the business or product is all about in a way that connects with the potential customer.

What is Christianity? We need to have a response ready for several reasons. First, we need to know ourselves what we believe. Second, we need to be able to recognize and challenge counterfeit Christianity, which in every age has wrought havoc in the church. We want the real thing, not a sham. Third, we need to be able to share with others what is dear to us. As the New Testament says, "always be ready to make your defense to anyone who demands from you an accounting for the hope that is in you; yet do it with gentleness and reverence" (1 Peter 3:15).

So we ask, what is Christianity? What is it in its essence? What would you answer on your elevator ride?

The New Testament's Answer

John knew nothing of elevators, but he answered this question succinctly in the first few verses of the New Testament book we call 1 John. What is Christianity? Christianity, quite simply, is Christ. Christianity is Christ, or it is counterfeit. We are the ones who through 2,000 years of Christianity history have often made that answer complicated and, indeed, have often obscured it.

Christianity is Christ. That's the elevator speech. I acknowledge that I want to take you on a skyscraper-height elevator ride, though, to explain it a bit more.

Christianity is Christ. It centers in him. This would seem to be a self-evident truth, but we often forget this truth.

Christianity is founded on the mind-stretching, earth-shaking truth than in a span of about thirty-three years, almost 2,000 years ago, in an insignificant little backwater of a Roman-dominated country in the Middle East, there lived a man named Jesus from a town called Nazareth. That's pretty ordinary, but get this. Christianity says that in this man named Jesus, God—the God of the universe—was present in a unique and special way. God came to us in this person Jesus. God came to us in a human life, not in philosophical propositions and ideas.

We call this truth the incarnation, which means God being in human flesh. We believe, against all logic, that this man Jesus was fully human and also fully God. He was fully human, but he was also as much of God as could get into a human life. Perhaps we can do no better with this mystery than to say with Paul that "in Christ God was reconciling the world to himself" (2 Corinthians 5:19).

This is the truth we have received and to which we witness. We must not err by thinking that Jesus was just a man—just human. Jesus was not simply a great human being, although he was a great human being. No, God himself was present in Jesus in a unique way.

The church councils and the theologians have spent centuries and many heated, complicated words trying to say what was involved in that unique way. Let us just hear the witness recorded in the New Testament.

At Jesus' baptism, God had declared through "a voice . . . from heaven, 'You are my Son, the Beloved; with you I am well pleased" (Mark 1:11). At Jesus' crucifixion, a Roman military man watched Jesus die and said, "Truly this man was God's Son!" (Mark 15:39).

Jesus' closest followers often seemed not to understand and had to be convinced themselves. Even so, they were convinced at last that Jesus was the Son of God. Thomas, the disciple whose skepticism is recorded in the most obvious way, finally said to Jesus, "My Lord and my God!" (John 20:28).

Jesus himself sensed this unique relationship with God. Jesus said during his ministry, "All things have been handed over to me by my Father; and no one knows the Son except the Father, and no one knows the Father except the Son and anyone to whom the Son chooses to reveal him" (Matthew 11:27).

The very life of Jesus also bore witness to his divinity. He, of all the great people who ever lived, practiced fully what he preached. He said, *Turn the other cheek*, and he did (Matt. 5:39). He taught, "Love your neighbor as yourself" (Matt. 22:39), and he did.

We err when we do not see Jesus for who he was—Lord and Savior, Son of God. He was the human being in whom God was uniquely present.

We may err in another way, too, about Jesus. We can err by not believing Jesus was really human. Many in that day felt that Jesus could not really be human, because in their view it was bad to be a fleshly human being. The divine could never really be associated with material things. The word of the Scriptures, though, is that "the Word became flesh and lived among us" (John 1:14). Further, as our text says, "what we have heard, what we have seen with our eyes, what we have looked at and touched with our hands, concerning the word of life—this life was revealed, and we have seen it and testify to it" (1 John 1:1-2). One of the reasons 1 John was written was to combat the false teaching that Jesus was not a human being.

It is not easy for us to think of Jesus as human. It is hard for us to think of him as a man with an ordinary occupation. It is hard for us to think of him as a carpenter, who maybe struck his thumb with his hammer sometime. But the witness of the New Testament is that Jesus was human, born as a baby. He needed to grow and mature as babies, children, youth, and adults do. He was tempted, as we are. He was limited in knowledge, as he himself said. He was fully human, like us, except for sin.

This is the most astonishing message of all time, that God came in human flesh. Jesus' contemporaries were enraged to hear it. We can hardly believe it ourselves. But here is where we must begin when we ask, *What is Christianity?* Christianity is Christ, God in human flesh.

What This Truth Means for Us

What difference does this elevator response make in a practical way for us? It means that God really cares about people, about us, about you.

God cared enough to come from heaven to be with us in Christ. God might have issued a statement, a news report, or a set of philosophical ideas, saying that he was really interested in us and cared about us. But that wasn't what God did. God came to us himself in Jesus of Nazareth to show us how much he cares for us. In Jesus, God became like us, except for our sin, in order that we might receive and live the abundant life that comes from God alone.

God does not have to guess about the human situation, about our needs, about your troubles and mine. God knows all about such things, first-hand.

Imagine a tragedy like an earthquake, a tornado, or a hurricane striking some far-off place. People were killed; cities were destroyed. How does that news strike you? Perhaps you have some sorrow and concern. Most likely, though, your concern is pretty limited, truth be told.

Unless—unless you have been to that place, unless you used to live there, unless you have family there, unless you have friends there. When you've been somewhere or know someone there personally, your interest and concern are heightened.

Well, God has been here. He has strong ties here. God's Son lived and died here. So we can know that God cares for us. As the New Testament says, "For we do not have a high priest who is unable to sympathize with our weaknesses, but we have one who in every respect has been tested as we are" (Hebrews 4:15). This is what God's coming in Christ means to us in a very practical way. God gets it. God gets what our lives are like, and God cares for us.

God's coming in Christ also means that God wants to have fellowship with us. God does not want to keep himself at a distance from us. God wants to share himself with us, and God wants for us to share ourselves with him.

There's an old story of a Persian king who took off his royal robes, dressed himself almost in rags, and went down into a tiny cellar where a poor man worked to keep the furnace burning for a large building. The king ate a meal with the poor man and became his friend. One day the king revealed who he really was. When the man was able at last to speak, he said, *You left your palace and your glory to sit with me in this place. You became my friend. You have given me the greatest gift of all. You have given me yourself.*

In Christ, God has given us himself. He has come to enter into fellowship with us, to share our concerns and our joys, to enrich our lives with his presence, and to offer us eternal fellowship with him. God's great love would not permit him the luxury of living at a distance from us. Thus God wants to have fellowship with us, and God wants us to experience this fellowship with him through faith.

The extent of this fellowship is more than just God and we as individuals alone, though. As we experience this freeing fellowship with God, we are led out of ourselves toward other people. We become bound together with God and with God's people in a fellowship of concern and love for one another and for all people. The incarnation means that God wishes to have fellowship with us, and it means further that God wishes us to participate in his fellowship with all people.

The coming of God in Christ means something else, too. John wrote, "We are writing these things so that our joy may be complete" (1 John

1:4). God's coming in Christ means joy. Shouldn't we be joyful to know that God cares for us? Shouldn't we be joyful that God wants to have fellowship with us? And shouldn't we be joyful at the possibilities for the tangled relationships of our world if we could somehow make God's kind of love supreme in our relationships with other people? And shouldn't we be joyful to know that God wishes us to have this joy throughout all eternity? How could we not be?

What to Do Next

There's an old story about a letter supposedly found decades ago in a remote part of the West. The letter was found in a can wired to the handle of an old pump at a well. The well was located on a very long and seldom-used trail across the desert. That well was the only hope of finding drinking water on that trail. The letter read like this:

> This pump is all right as of June 1932. I put a new . . . washer into it and it ought to last 5 years. But the washer dries out and the pump has got to be primed. Under the white rock I buried a bottle of enough water, out of the sun and cork end up. There's enough water in it to prime the pump, but not if you drink some first. Pour about one fourth and let her soak to wet the leather. Then pour in the rest medium fast and pump like crazy. You'll git water. The well has never run dry. Have faith. When you git watered up, fill the bottle and put it back like you found it for the next feller. (signed) Desert Pete

P.S. Don't go drinking up the water first. Prime the pump with it and you'll git all you can hold.[23]

Within this note from Desert Pete are some guidelines for what to do next after this elevator speech on Christianity. First, you place your faith in an unseen Person, Jesus, trusting that what the Person tells is true and will work. Second, you risk your life believing that more life really is available than what you can just grab for yourself. Third, you do what Jesus says.

Then you discover that there really is water, life, readily available. Life really is available through Christ, more life than you can hold. It's so good you don't just drink it up for yourself. Rather, you share it with others, however you can.

That's what Christianity is, and the elevator speech is that Christianity is Christ. Is this your kind of Christianity? Does it center in Christ? Through it, do you experience the care, fellowship, and joy of God himself? If this is your kind of Christianity, then you know that it came to you by faith. This kind of faith is the kind that makes you do something about what you say you believe and that you just can't keep to yourself.

10.

Acts 8:26-40
Witness? Who, Me?

Fifth Sunday of Easter

Someone has suggested that the average Christian has been listened to 4,000 sermons, heard 8,000 public prayers, sung 20,000 hymns and gospel songs, and given a verbal witness of his or her faith to 0 people. There's no evidence that much research went into all of these numbers. Too, the figures probably are inflated, given the norms of church attendance these days. But do you suppose they could be close to accurate—particularly the item about given a verbal witness of our faith?

I suspect there are several reactions to this opening statement. One might be genuine interest. A second might be guilt, for many of us have heard through the years that we ought to be witnesses for Christ. Frankly, though, that's not our thing. A third might be boredom, for we've heard something like that before. We're turning off the rest of the sermon right about now. A fourth might be resentment. We don't like the *E* word—evangelism—and we certainly don't like to hear anything about the *W* word—witnessing.

The purpose of giving our attention to this passage and offering this message on it, though, is to be helpful—not to cause guilt and certainly not resentment. The purpose is to lead us to consider what seems to have been second nature to the early church—telling others about Jesus and what Jesus had done for them. If we resent and resist the *E* word and the *W* word, we're going to have to ask ourselves how we justify to ourselves resenting and resisting this integral feature of the life of our early Christian brothers and sisters.

I share this message as a fellow pilgrim with you, for I also struggle with how to be faithful in sharing a verbal witness about my faith. I acknowledge that in our cultural circumstances and because of our individual personalities, it may not be easy for most of us. I say that as a certifiable introvert. But I'd like for us to see that finding appropriate ways to witness of our faith is a necessary ingredient for our living the abundant life Christ wants us to live.

Why Witnessing Is Important for Living the Abundant Life

So how can we dare to say that witnessing is important for living the abundant life in Christ? I think the answer is found in recognizing that living the best kind of life involves two big things—loving God and loving one's neighbor. I hope you will agree, for so Jesus affirmed in the two great commandments—love God and love your fellow human beings (Matthew 22:24-39). Let's look at these two commandments.

Witnessing is important because if we say inside ourselves that we love God, then that will come out in what we say and what we do. Not to talk about what means most to us may well block our growth and keep us from meaningful relationships with other people.

Have you ever had big, good news that you couldn't share yet? Maybe you had received a promotion but it wasn't public yet. Maybe you were pregnant but didn't want to announce it yet. Likely you felt as if you were not quite being honest and open even with people with whom you were friends. So, with this big, good news filling your mind, you talked about trivialities. You were blocked from the happiness and joy of sharing. Maybe you felt a little like a traitor.

Such experiences have some relationship to our sharing the good news of Christ. Not to share this good news diminishes us as people. It blocks our growth. It hinders our free and open relationship with other people.

Witnessing is also necessary because love for other people demands it. Imagine a doctor withholding a prescription for bringing healing.

Some of us recall the terror and worry of the days when polio ravaged the lives of children and adults. Then Dr. Jonas Salk discovered the vaccine, and we went as individuals, families, and groups to clinics to receive it in a little sugar cube. What if Dr. Salk had kept that discovery to himself for his own intellectual satisfaction, for his own health alone, or for the health of his family alone? If we had found out about it as people continued to be paralyzed and die because of polio, we would have been anything but happy with him.

Our love for people makes witnessing a necessity, too. The message of Jesus is what people need. Love compels us to share it.

Witnessing is also necessary because the best life is a life that is obedient to God's purposes. A part of that obedience is found in such passages as Matthew 28:18-20 and Acts 1:8. These passages are about witnessing, about sharing our faith. We are commanded to be Christ's witnesses. We are *sent* people.

Philip was just the kind of person we are talking about. He genuinely loved God, and he genuinely loved people.

Philip was what we would call a layperson. We first find him in Acts 6 as one of the seven church servants selected to minister to the Greek widows in the church. We next find him sharing the gospel with people many of his acquaintances in Jerusalem would have looked down on, the Samaritans (Acts 8). In our Scripture text, we find him telling a foreigner about Jesus. This foreigner would have been considered an outcast because of his physical condition, just as the Samaritans were outcasts because of their race and culture. But Philip shows us that witnessing is important for living the abundant life and for helping others to live such a life themselves.

How Can We Witness?

We may be reluctant to share a verbal witness because of many reasons. One of them surely is the bad experiences we have had or have known about with people who claimed they were witnessing but were really being high-powered manipulators. To this day, I want to get away as quickly as possible when such a person starts in my direction. Another reason perhaps is that we do not want to intrude on others' lives. Both of these are good reasons for proceeding cautiously. Look how Philip did it, though.

In verse 26, Philip got his instructions from an angel. In verse 29, it was the Spirit who encouraged him. Probably you might say, *Okay, well, sure, if an angel told me to do something or I was sure it was God's Spirit telling me, I'd probably do it. But since I don't believe I hear from such sources, I'll wait until I do. Fair enough?*

Yes, fair enough, but only if you are *willing* to listen and respond to God's promptings in your inner life. Often we don't listen and so we don't respond when God is prompting us to speak or act so as to point people to Christ. Interestingly, as Philip responded, he found the Ethiopian government official ready to engage in conversation.

Philip's experience here shows that witnessing is not telling how wonderful we are but sharing how gracious God has been to us in our need. An attitude of supposed holiness on our part is a barrier to witnessing. The true point of contact in having a conversation with people about sacred matters is our mutual need.

There is another part to the *how* of witnessing. We are to talk about the meaning of faith with overflowing concern and love for other people. Our experience with God is to help us love others, or what good is it? When we look at Philip's background, we see that he likely had had to grow in his love for people, all people.

Philip was a Greek-speaking Jew. In Jewish culture in the first century, Hellenists, Jews with a Greek background, were not as high on the social scale as Hebraic Jews, Jews with a Hebrew background. One of the reasons Philip was chosen as one of the seven to serve the Jerusalem church was to represent the Hellenist Jews who had become Christians. Next we find Philip going to the Samaritans and then to this Ethiopian who had been to Jerusalem to worship but was shut out of full worship of God because he had a physical condition that differed from the norm.

Perhaps Philip was so able to love these different people because he knew where he had come from. He knew what it was like to be looked down on, to not quite fit. But he also knew the difference Christ had made in his life.

So Philip was open to the needs of other people and sought ways to minister to them. Philip did not promote himself. As a result of the persecution that arose after Stephen's martyrdom, Philip went to Samaria to tell the good news of Christ there. Then he later joined the Ethiopian's chariot to try to answer the

Ethiopian's questions. In both cases, he was simply there to help. We, like Philip, are to be receptive to helping other people. We go not as holy people who somehow are above them but as fellow sinners and fellow sufferers. An old definition of evangelism is this: *Evangelism is one hungry beggar telling another where to find food.* And there's a lot of truth in that.

Philip shows another part of the how of witnessing. He witnessed faithfully to the gospel. Verse 35 states, "he proclaimed to him the good news about Jesus."

We may not know all the theology we think we need to know. Trust me; nobody does. But can't we just tell someone "the good news about Jesus" and what Jesus means to us? And we can keep learning more so we can be more confident in our sharing.

Too, we can live so as to validate our witness. At least our lives should not invalidate our witness. The most important part of this validation must be that we show love rather than try to overpower someone with our knowledge or otherwise engage in manipulation. "Above all, maintain constant love for one another, for love covers a multitude of sins," so 1 Peter 4:8 says. We will probably make many mistakes in sharing our faith, but showing genuine love has a way of moving the conversation beyond our mistakes. Right living matters, but loving deeds matter more. Acts of loving concern can open the way for conversation.

Who? Me?

Our early Christian brothers and sisters spread the Christian faith across the Roman Empire. Yes, there were preachers and scholars among them, but it happened largely through the witness of ordinary laypeople in their words and in their lives. They spoke about Christ and lived for Christ among the people whose lives they touched each day. For them, church gatherings were not mere religious club meetings shut off from life but were launch pads and refueling stations for lives of ministry and witness.

Granted, our cultural situation is different, but there are still opportunities. Let us show our love for God and for other people by being open and responsive to opportunities to share our faith.

11.

1 John 4:7-21
What the World Needs Now
Fifth Sunday of Easter

There's a story of a little girl who was being reared in a children's home. Her parents were gone, and her living with other relatives didn't work out. One day she was seen to hurry across the lawn and down a little hill to a tree. There she stopped. She looked around carefully to make sure to herself that no one had followed her or observed her. Then she knelt, lifted a rock, placed something under it, and went quickly back to the cottage where she lived.

But someone did notice what she had done. After the child had disappeared back into the building, the person who saw this went to the tree and lifted the rock to see what the little girl had placed under it. It was a folded piece of paper. She unfolded the paper and read these words, written in a child's scrawl: "Whoever you are, I love you."

That little story, true or not, shows us many things. For one, it shows us the resilience, the strength, of the human spirit. It reminds us, too, of when some of us have felt lonely and abandoned ourselves. Perhaps most touching, this little story also lets us see in action a single, frail, little human being doing the thing for which she was made—expressing love. She rose above her own lack and performed this beautiful act. "Whoever you are, I love you."

Much of the central meaning of the gospel, God's beautiful act of love on our behalf in sending Christ, comes through in this story. Through Christ, God says to us, "Whoever you are, I love you." As this text shows us, the good news for us also reminds us of our need to be loving people ourselves.

Of course, the love to which the text refers is the kind of love represented by the Greek word *agape*. This kind of love is God's kind of love. It is unlimited. It is for the unlovely as well as the lovely. It is for the people we think are like us, but it is also for the people we don't think are like us. It is for the people we don't like, and it is for the people who don't like us. It is unselfish concern for such people expressed in practical ways. It is the kind of love we see in God's clearest revelation of himself in Jesus.

The first letter of John is not written in a logical, point-by-point fashion, as we are used to reading. It has a definite structure, though. We might think of the structure of 1 John as being shaped like a coil spring, a spiral. The letter speaks about a theme, and then later it comes back to the theme, and then again and again.

First John does this as it talks about love. As it does, it gives us several important insights about love. We look at three of them.

Love Is Required

First, love is required. That's right. Love is not an option, but it is required of a Christian. Not loving is not being like Jesus. If you want to pick and choose in your love, to that extent you simply are not a follower of Jesus. If you are a Christian, you have no choice other than to love. Love is required.

This letter even says that love is a commandment. Follow the spiral backward from our text, and you will find these words:

> Beloved, I am writing you no new commandment, but an old commandment that you have had from the beginning; the old commandment is the word that you have heard. Yet I am writing you a new commandment that is true in him and in you, because the darkness is passing away and the true light is already shining. Whoever says, "I am in the light," while hating a brother or sister, is still in the darkness (1 John 2:7-9).

It is just that way with 1 John. Not loving means being in darkness. This symbol means being away from God, who is light.

The Gospel of John has a similar statement: "I give you a new commandment, that you love one another. Just as I have loved you, you also should love one another" (John 13:34).

So we have no choice but to love, if we are to be obedient Christians. Doesn't this commandment kind of gall you sometimes?

Really, doesn't it? Just when you'd like to go kick someone in the shin or elsewhere, a little light comes on way back there in the darkness of your mind. In glowing letters these words appear: "Whoever says, 'I am in the light,' while hating a brother or sister, is still in the darkness" (1 John 2:9).

We may not like it. In fact, the part of ourselves that is far from being like Jesus hates it. But there it is—a commandment and a dividing line, no less. This is not to say that we ought to deny our feelings when someone does something we feel is wrong or wrongs us directly. It is to say, though, that we need to learn to handle our feelings in a healthy way and, if possible, learn to love. Truly, that's tough sometimes, isn't it? But we are still commanded to love. And the Christian has someone—the Holy Spirit—to help us keep the commandment to love.

So love is required, and it is required because of a commandment. But there's more. It is also required because of a relationship. Listen to some verses about this idea that spiral up from 1 John:

> This is the message we have heard from him and proclaim to you, that God is light and in him there is no darkness at all. If we say that we have fellowship with him while we are walking in darkness, we lie and do not do what is true (1:5-6).

> Whoever loves a brother or sister lives in the light, and in such a person there is no cause for stumbling. But whoever hates another believer is in the darkness, walks

in the darkness, and does not know the way to go, because the darkness has brought on blindness (2:10-11).

We must not be like Cain who was from the evil one and murdered his brother. And why did he murder him? Because his own deeds were evil and his brother's righteous (3:12).

We know love by this, that he laid down his life for us—and we ought to lay down our lives for one another (3:16).

Beloved, since God loved us so much, we also ought to love one another (4:11).

So we have known and believe the love that God has for us. God is love, and those who abide in love abide in God, and God abides in them (4:16).

These verses suggest that our relationship with God *requires* that we love. Even more, our relationship with God *inspires* us to love.

Is there someone in your life who loves you and whose life inspires you also to love? You would not want to disappoint them for anything. When we truly recognize God's love for us in Jesus, then we do not want to do anything that disregards or tarnishes that love. In fact, because of that relationship, we want to pass that love along to others.

Love is required, too, because of the consequences. Not to love is self-destructive, as 1 John 2:11 states: "But whoever hates another believer is in the darkness, walks in the darkness, and does not know the way to go, because the darkness has brought on blindness." We blind ourselves when we refuse to love.

Further, when we refuse to love, we remain in death and darkness, apart from the abundant life Jesus offers. "We know that we have passed from death to life because we love one another. Whoever does not love abides in death" (3:14).

Who benefits when we refuse to love because of some wrong we feel someone has done to us? We certainly don't. We cut ourselves off from the truly good life.

But to love—that is creative. It enables us to see. It enables us to live. It enables us to give life to others.

As 1 John spirals forth its message about love, it says a second important thing about it.

Love Is Practical

John just will not let us off the hook when he talks about love. Not only does John say it is required, but he also says that this love is practical, and very much so. He won't let us just talk about it and philosophize about it.

John says that love has to be concerned about the person we see.

> Those who say, "I love God," and hate their brothers or sisters, are liars; for those who do not love a brother or sister whom they have seen, cannot love God whom they have not seen. The commandment we have from him is this:

those who love God must love their brothers and sisters also (4:20-21).

John won't let us just get all exercised about people 10,000 miles away without seeing that we need to love the people around us—the people with whom we walk the sidewalks and drive the streets. Certainly we must be concerned with the people far away, but we must not use that concern to forget those near to us. We must be concerned for all people—whether they are rich, poor, or in-between; whether the person's face is dark or light; whether we think the person is of our tribe or not; whether the person's personality is pretty rough or fairly likable. The person we see—John wants us to love that person.

A Christian young woman was invited to speak to a group of even younger women who were in prison. She went, reluctantly. She talked about what sinners they were. There was not much love in what she said. It was the last place on earth she wanted to be. Her audience was hardly appreciative, either. She lost them after the first couple of sentences. She left feeling she was an utter failure.

Somehow, though, she was invited back a few months later. Maybe they couldn't get anyone else to come. Anyway, this time she decided to talk about God's love for them. The reason was that this woman herself somehow during the intervening time had become willing to love these young women even though they were outcasts. She had changed. She had come to realize that these young women were still people God loved.

She saw them like that, and she knew she was to love them herself, too.

A friend of mine had a similar ministry to women in prison. She went regularly to talk with the women. She loved God, and she knew how to show love to these women. They adored her and learned from her. Lives were changed because of Jo's love.

Love is exceedingly practical, says John. "How does God's love abide in anyone who has the world's goods and sees a brother or sister in need and yet refuses help? Little children, let us love, not in word or speech, but in truth and action" (3:17-18).

The Source of Love

Where do we get the strength and the wisdom to show this kind of creative, practical love? John says that the place to get this kind of love is the God who is love.

We don't get this kind of love by gritting our teeth and bearing with some troublesome person. We get resentment.

We don't get this kind of love by avoiding people. We get withdrawn into a shell, and we become more and more unfeeling and unloving ourselves. Yes, I admit that as a survival strategy we may need to distance ourselves from a toxic person, a person who takes advantage of our kindness. Sometimes the person has the porcupine quills out to inflict harm, and we need to keep our distance because we see no way to show love.

But let us always be seeking to love. Where do we get this kind of love? We get this kind of love from God, who makes us his children. "See what love the Father has given us, that we should be called children of God; and that is what we are" (3:1). Further, "since God loved us so much, we also ought to love one another" (4:11).

The gospel always leads us back to this truth, doesn't it? We get love to show to other people only by receiving the God who is love into our hearts and lives. The source of our love for others—and even for ourselves—is God's love for us. "In this is love, not that we loved God but that he loved us and sent his Son to be the atoning sacrifice for our sins. Beloved, since God loved us so much, we also ought to love one another" (4:10-11). That's the gospel truth.

12.

John 15:9-17
A Good Church

Sixth Sunday of Easter

What is an ideal church? Forget ideal. What is a *good* church? Sometimes we speak of a certain church as being "a good church." We may even use those words to describe our own church. But what do we mean? What do we look for in a good church, even an ideal church?

If we tell the truth about it, likely we look for those things that satisfy our own ideas and tastes. If we feel that *a good church* means hearing a certain kind of preaching and a certain kind of music, likely we call the church good that has that sort of preaching and music. If we feel that church means a beautiful sanctuary, tastefully decorated, that is what we look for. If we feel that a good church is one that has friendly people in it, we look for that and are impressed when we find it.

There probably are many standards we could use to define a good church. Do we have the right standards, though? Are we asking the right questions? Do we evaluate other churches and our own in the right way? What really makes a good church, even an ideal church?

Before Jesus went to the cross, he spent much time instructing and preparing his disciples. On the last evening of his earthly life before the cross, Jesus spoke to the disciples in a pointed way about who he was, who they were to be, and what they were to do.

The verses in the text were spoken at that time. They will go a long way in helping us understand what Christ's ideal church is like and how our church can be like that.

Created by Christ

One way to evaluate a church is to try to discover its source—where it came from and how it came into existence. This means more than who its founders were and more even than how a group of people came together to be called a church. It means that, but it goes further.

Where did the church come from? How did it come into existence? Even more pointed, what is the source of its life?

There's a lot of talk these days about being spiritual but not being religious, about being spiritual but not bothering with the church. Jesus, though, elevated the importance of the church with this statement: "You did not choose me but I chose you" (John 15:16). This statement is a reminder that the source of the church is Jesus himself.

The disciples were a motley crew. They had many differences. The main thing that joined them together was that Christ had chosen them and they had responded to that choice. Could we say the same thing about ourselves?

The reality is that the people in most churches these days have lots of things in common. Perhaps it's geographical proximity, perhaps it's ethnicity, perhaps it's income, perhaps it's education, perhaps it's social strata.

There's not necessarily anything wrong with any of these qualities characterizing most of the church members. There *is* something wrong if one or more of these qualities becomes the spoken or unspoken entrance requirement for a church, though. There is something wrong if people not like us are shut out and unwelcome. We ought to be doing everything we can to break down as many human barriers as we can and to become a truly inclusive church.

In a good church—Christ's ideal church— people are together in a group worthy of the name "church" when they know that Christ himself has called them to be a member of it. Furthermore, they do not use any of their human or cultural qualities to stay in the church or to keep other people out of it.

They know that on their own they could not have created the church. They know that they owe their existence as a church to God in Christ himself and not to human and cultural qualities on their own. On their own, the members of such a church—a good church—could not really have even "joined" the church. They could join the organization, but not the church.

Why? Christ's ideal church is created by Christ and by no other. Christ is the source of the church's life and nothing else. Only Christ creates a good church.

Who do we say created our church? Do we point back to the founders? Do we point back to the people who preceded us? Do we point back to some leader or leaders? Do we look around at ourselves and say, *We did it?* Or do we point to Christ? An ideal church, even a good church, with humility knows that Christ created it and that it is Christ to whom they owe their gratitude and allegiance.

"You did not choose me but I chose you" (15:16). Yes, that's the way it was in the upper room, and that is the way it needs to be with us.

Commissioned to Serve Christ

A good church is also one that has been commissioned by Christ and is carrying out that commission. A good church is on mission, on Christ's mission. Jesus said, "I appointed you to go and bear fruit, fruit that will last. . . " (15:15).

A church is not a religious association that meets weekly to meditate about religious ideas. No, a church is a people who have a commission from the Creator of the church that we should "go and bear fruit, fruit that will last . . . ." That is, our individual lives and the church's life together should be productive for the Master's sake.

You likely have heard often the old question, "Are you a part of the problem or a part of the answer?" The Christian and the church are duty-bound to be part of the answer in every situation of which they are a part. They are to go and bear fruit. That is their commission and ours.

Our lives and our words are to contribute to people being helped to find God's answer to their immediate and ultimate needs. We are to be people of "love, joy, peace, patience, kindness, generosity, faithfulness, gentleness, and self-control" (Galatians 5:22). We are to spend our lives and our resources in bringing wholeness of life to people. This is the only fruit that lasts, the fruit that grows in the lives of people.

In Constant Touch with Christ

In this text, Jesus' words to his disciples on the last night of his earthly life show us another quality of Christ's ideal church. Christ's ideal church, his good church, is constantly in touch with him, with the One who gives strength to do his work.

We are to "ask" the Father "in [Jesus'] name" that he may give us what is needed (John 15:16). We are to be in touch with God through our Lord Jesus Christ. The strength out of which we live is to be Christ's strength.

How do we live physically? Sometimes we feel as if it is we ourselves who make us live, or at least we may take our lives pretty much for granted. But how do we live? Try going without food, water, air. We could not live. We live only through what we take into ourselves to fill our needs.

A church lives, too, only by how much of God it takes into itself. On its own, a church cannot live. A good church lives in the power of God, not out of its own power. God provides the strength for a good church's life. We receive this strength by staying in touch with God through prayer, through Bible study, through obedience, and through being where God is at work in the world and working with God there.

Earlier in this chapter and earlier in that evening, Jesus had this to say about this theme:

> Abide in me as I abide in you. Just as the branch cannot bear fruit by itself unless it abides in the vine, neither can you unless you abide in me. I am the vine, you are the branches. Those who abide in me and I in them bear much fruit, because apart from me you can do nothing. Whoever does not abide in me is thrown away like a branch and withers; such branches are gathered, thrown into the fire, and burned. If you abide in me, and my words abide in you, ask for whatever you wish, and it will be done for you (15:4-7).

An ideal church, even a good church, is constantly in touch with God. It does not act on its own. It does not even justify its actions by claiming they are God's. Rather it humbly lives its life out of God's life, seeking God's way rather than its own.

Caring for People

Christ's ideal church has yet another characteristic—love. His ideal church, even a good church, cares for people. On that last night, Jesus said, "This is my commandment, that you love one another as I have loved you. No one has greater love than this, to lay down one's life for one's friends" (15:12-13).

A good church cares for people. No matter how many programs a church has, it fails when it does not care for people. No matter how much money it has, how much money it gives to missions, how many mission trips it takes, or how many baptisms it reports, a church fails unless it cares for people. Of course, a church can express its concern for people in all of these ways and more—programs, finances, members, baptisms, and so on—but such things are suspect unless a church cares for people.

If a church cares more for itself as an institution than it cares for people, it is not a good church. Indeed, it may not even be a church, no matter what the sign on the front says.

This is so with individuals, too. We ourselves may not be able to meet every need of every person, but we ought to be seeking to do that.

A good church's inner relationships are characterized by concern for one another. We are to be mutual burden-bearers. We are to be slow to take offense and eager for reconciliation. We are to be true friends and not just friendly.

A good church's outer relationships aim at caring for people in all of their needs. "Love one another"—so our Lord told the disciples that night (15:17). So our Lord tells us, too.

Likely we could name other things that go into making a good church, but surely these things would be on the list, too—created by Christ, commissioned to serve Christ, in constant touch with God, caring for people. We ought to measure a good church by such standards.

In one of the most relevant and at the same time painful services of worship in which I ever participated, the pastor asked, "Is our church a good church?" He paused for a long time. The room was filled with many people, but it was quiet. You could not even hear people breathing. I don't think they *were* breathing but rather just holding their breath. Because of the difficulties the church was experiencing, they all knew the answer to his question. He finally said it—"No." Everyone in the sanctuary knew he was right. It was a terrible thing to be said and heard. The word was true, though, and the word was needed. He continued, "But we can be." Then he proceeded to tell how.

Is your church a good church? If not, or if your church is not as good a church as it needs to be and can be, isn't it time it became one?

13.
Ezekiel 37:1-14
Hope in Death Valley
Day of Pentecost

The African-American spiritual "Dry Bones" captures well the excitement of this passage.[24] Perhaps you have sung it. Even if you haven't, you likely remember something about the toe bone being connected to the foot bone and the ankle bone being connected to the leg bone, and on and on upward. Both the spiritual and the Scripture passage are about new life and new hope.

Ezekiel probably is not the most familiar book in the Bible to many of us. In many ways it's an unusual book, filled with strange imagery. One problem we have with the Book of Ezekiel is the same problem we have with all the books of all the prophets. We think the prophets were interested only in the distant future, but that's not so. The prophets spoke the word of God to their own day. The prophets appealed for reform, warned of what would happen if the people didn't change, and often pronounced the promises of God if the reform was carried out.

Go down into the valley of dry bones, into death valley, with me. Most likely we will find we've been there ourselves along with Ezekiel, or we will be. Let us learn from his experience there.

What Happened Then?

In a vision, "the spirit of the LORD set" Ezekiel "down in the middle of a valley; it was full of bones" (Ezekiel 37:1). Ezekiel saw "there were very many lying in the valley, and they were very dry" (Ezek. 37:2). Later in the passage, God explained to Ezekiel that "these bones are the whole house of Israel. They say, 'Our bones are dried up, and our hope is lost; we are cut off completely'" (37:11). Israel's dead hopes were like the dry bones in the valley.

A few years before, in 598 BC, the part of Israel called Judah had been defeated soundly by the Babylonian army. The king, his mother, other government officials, the leading citizens, and much of the nation's wealth had been taken to Babylon.

About ten years later, in 588 BC, the nation revolted against Babylon. This time things would be even worse. Babylon would have no mercy. The Babylonian army destroyed Jerusalem, executed the nation's leaders, and took many people into exile.

Judah felt its hope for the future had been destroyed. They were a conquered and exiled people. Psalm 137 captures the anguish they felt.

By the rivers of Babylon—
    there we sat down and there we wept

when we remembered Zion.
On the willows there
We hung up our harps.

For there our captors
asked us for songs,
And our tormentors asked for mirth,
saying,
"Sing us one of the songs of Zion!"
How could we sing the LORD's song
in a foreign land?

Their hopes were like dry bones. Their chances of recovering seemed to be exactly none.

Their hopelessness is shown further in verse 3 of our text. The Spirit asked Ezekiel, "Can these bones live?" Ezekiel could only reply, "O Lord GOD, you know." Ezekiel's response means that the situation seemed hopeless to him. Any hope had to come from God.

Then God took Ezekiel a step further. The Spirit commanded Ezekiel to do an outrageous thing. The Spirit said (Ezek. 37:4-6),

Prophesy to these bones, and say to them: O dry bones, hear the word of the LORD. Thus says the Lord GOD to these bones: I will cause breath to enter you, and you shall live. I will lay sinews on you, and will cause flesh to come upon you, and cover you with skin, and put breath in you, and you shall live; and you shall know that I am the LORD.

Ezekiel obeyed, and here comes the background to the African-American spiritual song. "There was a noise, a rattling, and the bones came together, bone to its bone. I looked, and there were sinews on them, and flesh had come upon them, and skin had covered them" (37:7-8).

One thing was missing. Don't worry, though. God supplied that, too. What was missing was breath, spirit, life. When Ezekiel prophesied further as God commanded, "the breath came into them, and they lived, and stood on their feet, a vast multitude" (37:10).

We see the meaning of this event in verses 12-14. Ezekiel was to preach to the hopeless exiles in Babylon that there was hope. God was going to raise them up out of their hopelessness. God would bring them out of the grave of exile and back to the land of Israel, their homeland. God did that, not too many years later.

The Meaning Now

What is the meaning for people like us as we reflect on God's actions then? The text puts its finger on part of the mood of our time and perhaps of our lives. Sometimes it seems we live in the midst of a great feeling of hopelessness. We may wonder what the world is coming to. There seem to be so many things that are not quite right that we wonder whether there is any hope.

We sometimes feel that way about our world. We sometimes feel that way about our nation. We sometimes feel that way about our families. We sometimes feel that way about our jobs. We sometimes feel that way about our church. We sometimes feel that way about ourselves.

The text shows us something else, though. If all we see is hopelessness, dry bones in death valley, we don't see enough. We don't see that there is hope.

One of the big reasons hopelessness is not right is that hopelessness does not take account of the greatness of God. Where there's God, there's hope. God can make dry bones and despairing people live. We sometimes feel God has the same reaction to difficult times as we have, that God's brow is furrowed with worry and that God is wringing his hands in heaven about what is going on. That is a mistake. We forget that God can make dry bones live.

To yield to a feeling of hopelessness betrays a lack of confidence and trust. In France, the skeptic Voltaire predicted that by the end of the eighteenth century the teachings of Christianity would be all but forgotten. About the same time, a cobbler in England was having different ideas. This cobbler named William Carey had a motto, "Expect great things from God; attempt great things for God." Everybody didn't agree with him, not even his fellow Christians, but soon that cobbler sailed to India to begin the modern missionary movement.

"Expect great things from God; attempt great things for God." Rather than be overcome by hopelessness, despair, and pessimism, Carey let this motto guide him. We would do well to follow his example. We must expect, and we must attempt. With God, there is hope.

The Application for Us

A little more specifically, how does this text apply to us? Because of what this Scripture tells us about both people and God, what will we need to do?

First, let us move away from the idea that we know what's going to happen to this world and our lives. God asked Ezekiel, "Can these bones live?" Ezekiel wisely replied, "You know" (37:3). That's our best response, too, if we say it more positively than Ezekiel did. The perennial pessimist puts a damper on the spirit of everyone. We need a brand of realism that recognizes the reality of whatever the situation is but that also doesn't forever dwell on the darkest side of it but rather looks for ways to work with whatever light there is. God can change situations that look hopeless.

Something else we need to do besides removing pessimism from our minds is to put our trust in God in and in spite of the circumstances. Such an approach does not require shutting our eyes to problems, but it does require daring to believe, as Romans 8:28 states, "We know that all things work together for good for those who love God. . . . " Or even as we can translate it, *We know that God works all things together for good for those who love him.* We trust in this kind of God.

A final application is that we will need to put our trust to work as Ezekiel did. At first glance in this passage of Scripture, it appears that God performs great things in spite of and without people. That is a legitimate emphasis of the Scriptures, but notice that God was using Ezekiel as his instrument. It was to Ezekiel's credit that he was receptive to hear God's voice, see God's vision, and take action as God commanded. So we ourselves are to do.

The old spiritual based on this passage says, "Dem bones, dem bones, they's gonna walk again. . . . I hear the word of the Lord." I think the song has something. I think the Scripture text has something. Let's hear and do the word of the Lord. He can make us walk again, although we may feel right now that all is hopeless. Because of God, there is hope, even in death valley.

14.

Isaiah 6:1-8
Just Say Yes

Trinity Sunday: First Sunday after Pentecost

Early on during the time I was working with the national Boy Scouts of America as director of Creative Services, we became involved in a process to improve our service to our customers. It's an intense process you might have been involved in yourself, since many corporations used it. It's called TQM—Total Quality Management. The process is aimed at continual improvement.

One of the editors in my organization came up with a brilliant slogan—"We Say Yes!" The slogan portrayed a positive change in attitude in how we dealt with our customers, and that attitude and all of the changes we made enabled us to move customer satisfaction percentage levels from the 70s to the high 90s.

"Yes" is a powerful word that opens up opportunities. Someone has suggested that the proper response to God is, "The answer is yes, Lord. What's the question?" So before we even find out what God's question to us is, our answer is *yes*.

The truth, however, is that few of us live like that. We tend to question God and what God wants us to do rather than answering God's question. We tend to move through life following our agenda instead of God's. Isaiah 6, however, encourages us to respond to God's call to us and suggests ways we can hear it and do it.

The Questions

So, if *yes* is the answer, what is the question? Actually, there are two of them. They fit every person.

The first question is, Will you say *yes* to God's call? What do we mean by God's call? We sometimes talk about being called to preach, being called to this or that occupation, or being called to do something specific. It's okay to talk like that, provided we don't let ourselves off the hook and think that one person is called but we are not.

In the New Testament, every person is called. The basic call is the call to be a Christian. Look all over the New Testament and you will not find the word "called" used except to refer to being called to be a Christian. So every person is called in that sense.

In our churches, we sometimes labor under a terrible and dangerous misconception. Somehow many have understood salvation to mean that one can be saved *by* Jesus without becoming a disciple *of* Jesus. Or that one can be a church member without being Jesus' disciple. Of course, it's possible for a person on his or her deathbed to turn to Jesus in faith and be saved. But if the person gets well, he or she had better live like it or the experience becomes just another foxhole conversion that turns out not to be real.

That is not the picture of Christianity that we get in the New Testament, particularly the Gospels. There salvation is simple. Salvation is hearing Jesus' invitation, saying to yourself and Jesus that Jesus' way is the right way, and getting up and following him. It is becoming Jesus' apprentice or student, learning from Jesus how to live. There is no two-tiered Christianity— one level for folks who just barely get into heaven and a higher level for people who are serious about the Christian life. Being saved means being Jesus' disciple.

Being saved is about saying *yes* to Jesus not just one time, but whenever the question comes up. Does that mean if one of those 100 times in a day you say *no* you're damned for eternity? No, God's grace is more powerful than that. It means, though, that the intention and focus of our lives must be to say *yes* to Jesus.

There's a second question, Will you say *yes* to God's sending you on a mission for him? If you've said *yes* to the first question, you are disobedient if you say *no* to the second one. Once you've said *yes* to God's call to be a Christian, the response to every question from God after that must be *yes*, not *no*. We are to "just say *yes*," not "just say *no*."

But here's the big question. Will we be obedient or disobedient? You've likely heard of the 80/20 rule. For example, a business gets 80 percent of its profit from 20 percent of its customers. Or a church gets 80 percent of its service, its gifts, from 20 percent of its members. Why is that so? Because some people are saying *no* when they should be saying *yes*.

Which percent are you in? This is a case where being in the majority is not a good thing, not good at all.

The message of the New Testament is that everyone is called to be a Christian. When you say *yes* to that call, you get three big gifts. You get the gift of salvation. As Romans 6:23 states, "For the wages of sin is death but the free gift of God is eternal life through Jesus Christ our Lord." Second, you get the Holy Spirit. As Romans 5:5 states, "God has poured out his love into our hearts by the Holy Spirit, whom he has given us." Third, you get at least one gift to use in service to God. As Romans 12:6 states, "We have different gifts, according to the grace given us." God gives you at least one gift, and that gift is to be used for others. It's not an option. God expects that you will "just say *yes*."

Learning to Say *Yes*

How can you be more receptive to God's call and God's sending? How can you learn to "just say *yes*" to God instead of either saying *no* or acting as if you didn't hear the question? This is where Isaiah helps us and helps us terrifically. The experience of Isaiah in this text models for us how God calls and sends us.

First, God calls through making us aware of the world's needs. Here we need a brief history lesson, and let me give it to you as quickly as I can and with a spoonful of sugar to help it go down. Isaiah 6:1 sets Isaiah's call in the context of Isaiah's world. It was not an accident or a coincidence that led Isaiah to hear God's call at this particular time. The year was 742 B.C., and the nation felt it was on shaky ground. King Uzziah, who had reigned for so long and so well, was dead. People who have lived through the sudden death of a president of the United States may be able to understand some of the feelings of the people of Judah in that circumstance. When King Uzziah died, they felt they had lost their moorings. They hoped that the next king, Jotham, Uzziah's son, would prove worthy, but they were concerned about how the nation would fare under King Jotham's leadership.

A second, larger problem loomed just over the horizon, though, the eastern horizon. Times of peace, prosperity, and expansion in Israel and Judah generally coincided with times when the nations on either side of them were weak. The Promised Land formed a sort of land bridge between two great centers of power—Egypt on one side and, on the other, whatever nation was in power in the area of the Tigris-Euphrates River.

During the reigns of King Uzziah in Judah and King Jeroboam in Israel, each of the two great centers on either side of them had been in a time of weakness. So Israel and Judah thrived. The times were changing, though. The Assyrian war machine was cranking up and was rumbling toward overrunning and destroying everything in its way. Israel and Judah were in the way.

In such a situation, God called Isaiah. A part of God's call to Isaiah likely was mediated through the needs of Isaiah's world. The times were troubling and promised to become even more troubling. Other passages in Isaiah show Isaiah's awareness of other aspects of these troubling times.

In addition to threats from without and concerns about leadership within, the people had strayed from God in how they worshiped and in how they treated their fellow citizens. Many of the same kinds of things that had been occurring in Israel were also occurring in Judah, the Southern kingdom. Greed, not God, tended to dominate the people's lives, and the powerful people mistreated the less powerful people in order to get gain.

Now that we've looked at some of the circumstances of Isaiah's world, what are the circumstances of your life? Of what needs are you aware, in your family, among your friends, in your church, and also in your community, at work, and in the larger world? The needs of which you are aware may be a part of God's call to you, a call God wants you to answer.

Let me tell you about something that happened in the first church I served out of seminary, in the very first few months of my being there. The nominating committee had asked everyone they could think of to serve as director of the older children's Sunday School. No one said *yes*; everyone said *no*. Everyone had good reasons, well, almost everyone. As the custom was in that day, the nominating committee presented its report to the church. There was a blank line beside the position of director of the older children's Sunday School. One person whom we'd asked but who had said *no* rose during the business meeting and said, "I can't stand to see that blank for the teacher for those precious children." On the spot she said *yes* and served wonderfully. When you know of a need, it may be God calling you.

How else does God call other than through the needs around us? A second answer is that God calls through a recognition of God's greatness. One reason we don't say *yes* to God is that we don't recognize God's greatness.

The scene Isaiah saw as described in verses 2-4 is magnificent. Isaiah perhaps was in a worship service at the temple when God revealed to Isaiah a scene grander than even the temple provided. God gave Isaiah a vision that enabled him to see into heaven itself.

What did Isaiah see? He saw a majestic vision of the Lord. The vision filled the temple. Isaiah saw and heard the seraphim, angelic creatures who ministered to the Lord. One called out to another in praise of God's holiness and noted that God's presence filled not just the temple but the world itself (6:3). In the scene, the temple shook and filled with smoke (6:4). The picture was awesome, and awe overcame Isaiah.

We likely will not care much about God's call, much less answer it, if we do not have a sense of God's greatness. If we do not sense God's awe-inspiring, overwhelming greatness, God's call becomes just another call in a cacophony of voices. We hear it, look at our calendar, decide we're too busy, pass it by, and forget it. Only when we recognize that God's call takes precedence over all other calls will we rearrange our calendars and lives for it.

Third, God also calls through an experience of God's grace. One reason we don't say *yes* to God's call is that we've forgotten how much we owe God. God saved our souls, yes, and God has saved us from harm and even catastrophe on many occasions.

Isaiah 6:5 tells how Isaiah reacted to his recognition of God's greatness. When Isaiah recognized God's holiness, Isaiah was moved immediately to recognize his sinfulness. A cry of woe emerged from Isaiah's heart. Isaiah knew his character was no match for God's character. Isaiah felt he was doomed because of his great sinfulness and because of the sinfulness of his people, of which he was a part. People like Isaiah who truly are close to the Lord do not tend to boast in their goodness but rather to confess their sinfulness.

Being made aware of our limitations, even of our sin, is painful, but it can be an experience from which we learn and through which we hear God speak. Furthermore, only when we recognize our need of God's grace can we receive God's grace.

The wonderful news of the Bible, though, is this: "If we confess our sins, he who is faithful and just will forgive us our sins and cleanse us from all unrighteousness" (1 John 1:9). Isaiah, who lived centuries earlier than when that verse in 1 John was written, could nevertheless testify to its truth. Isaiah 6:6-7 describes vividly God's extension of forgiveness to Isaiah. Now, said the seraph, "Your guilt has departed and your sin is blotted out" (Isa. 6:7).

Such an experience of God's grace is essential to our hearing and answering God's call. People who are boasting about themselves are unable to hear God, and hearing God is the prerequisite for answering God.

Fourth, God also calls through a focus on God's mission. Isaiah 6:8-12 outlines what happened next. Isaiah answered God's call. Actually, Isaiah overheard God talking with the heavenly council about God's mission. God was expressing a need for someone to send.

Isaiah did what may seem unthinkable. He didn't have to be persuaded; he volunteered to go. Isaiah so desired, out of gratitude for God's grace, to participate in God's mission that he volunteered without knowing exactly what the mission was going to be.

Isaiah only afterward found the difficulties that would lie ahead. For one thing, the people would not respond positively to the message. As a matter of fact, they would reject it. Furthermore, they would keep on rejecting it. God told Isaiah that he would not be successful in his assigned task.

This passage reminds us that the important thing is for us to get in line with God's mission. God, not us, will take care of the success or failure of God's mission. Our task is to hear and answer God's call.

Here is a fifth way in which we can hear God's call and go where God sends us—become aware of our gifts. Here's what the Bible says about gifts, in a nutshell: Every Christian has at least one. The source is God. We are to use them for building others up, not for calling attention to ourselves. We are to develop and use our gifts. God holds us accountable for doing that.

How can we become aware of our gifts? Look at what you're good at, what you like to do, and what you have the opportunity to do. You may need to experiment to find out if that's for you. A friend of mine thought he had the gift of playing the banjo. I'm not making this up. Thank God he found he didn't have that gift before it was too late and he subjected many of his friends to his supposed gift. If you *do* have the gift of playing the banjo, play on, especially if you play bluegrass!

A word of caution: you don't have to like what you are called to do in order actually to be called to do it. The prophet Jeremiah didn't like what God asked him to do. And I've been in a situation or two where I knew I was doing what I was supposed to do but I would rather have been somewhere else.

But it's still not a bad guide, with exceptions—what you're good at, what you like to do, what you have opportunity to do.

Will You "Just Say *Yes*" to God?

Look at Isaiah. Isaiah did the unthinkable. He said *yes* even before he knew the question. Are you willing to live like that? If not, you may not yet know the meaning of Jesus' words, "Follow me." You have not yet seen that if you said *yes* to God's call to be a Christian, you also said *yes* to God's plan to send you to do God's mission. I don't believe you can find in the New Testament that separation between being saved and being a disciple.

There are times in our lives it seems as if we wake up to what is happening in our lives and see more clearly than we have ever seen before. Sometimes that's in the transition times—when we move from high school to college or from college to the world of work; when a new baby comes; or when a child graduates from high school or college. Sometimes it's when something happens in our lives and suddenly we just wake up as if from a daze.

A successful small-town attorney in Kentucky woke up one day and realized God wanted him to do something special with his life. He believed God wanted him to be a Christian in his daily work and wanted him to help other people to do that. So he gathered a group of fellow attorneys and they started looking at how God wanted them to live. Some lives got changed, and some eyes got opened.

In my relationships, I try to operate out of what I call *isness* instead of *oughtness*. I don't feel a great need to tell people what they *ought* to do. Likely they have enough other people telling them that. I try to tell people how I believe it *is*. Then they get to decide for themselves. The Holy Spirit will lead them without me saying they *ought* to do something or not. That's what I mean by *isness*.

So consider these questions for yourself: First, have you said *yes* to God's call to be a Christian? Second, if you've said *yes* to God's call to be a Christian, have you said *yes* to God's mission? If not, how will you explain to God why you said *no* to God's mission? So I encourage you, "Just Say Yes."[25]

15.

1 Samuel 8:4-20
Be Wise about What You Want
Proper 5 (10): Second Sunday after Pentecost

An ancient story from India tells about three travelers who came to see a wise man. They wanted to inquire of him about how they might receive their greatest desire. Receiving their greatest desire, they believed, would then result in great happiness for each of them.

In the course of the meeting, the wise man promised to give each person his greatest desire. The first chose long life. The second chose great wealth. The third asked for great physical strength. Each one believed that receiving what he wanted would result in great happiness in life.

So the wise man granted each one his greatest desire. The result, though, was not good for any of them. Receiving what they most wanted did not result in happiness for any of them.

The first person, who had chosen long life, lived a long life but underwent great suffering for all of those many years. Happiness eluded him.

The second person, the one who chose great wealth, was greatly disliked by his neighbors and acquaintances and in the end was murdered. He was not happy about it.

The third person, the one who asked for great physical strength, was captured by his enemies and tortured. The torture lasted interminably long because of his great strength.

This third person and his two friends had gotten what they wanted, but things did not turn out as they expected. Getting what they wanted did not result in happiness.

In this incident in the life of ancient Israel, Samuel had been judge for a long time. He was getting old, and it had become hard for him to fulfill his duties. It was clear that he could not continue as judge much longer.

Samuel had two sons, but Israel's leaders did not want them to succeed Samuel. Samuel's sons had proven themselves to be like the previous priest's sons. They were corrupt.

So the elders proposed a solution to Samuel. That's what this passage and Samuel's response to the solution is about. The passage tells the story of a great transition in the life of ancient Israel. It has a message for us, too.

As with the elders of Israel, what we want, or what we think we want, or what we think is the best, may not turn out to be best or even nearly as good as we thought it would be. At the very least, there will be problems when we get what we want. That's certainly so when what we want is bad, but even predominantly good things may have problems inherent in them. So, the text tells us, be wise about what you let yourself want.

In the Background (7:1—8:3)

Look at the background to the incident in 1 Samuel 8:4-20. Verses 12-14 of 1 Samuel 7 focus on Samuel's service to God and to the people as a judge with judicial functions and as a deliverer. The story of the judges is in some ways epitomized in Samuel in this incident.

In chapters 5—6, the Philistines had captured the most sacred possession of Israel, the ark of the covenant. The people were in deep sorrow. In 1 Samuel 7, Samuel gathered the people and challenged them to repent. They did, and Israel was victorious over the Philistines. When the people had turned to the Lord, the Lord had delivered them from their enemies, the Philistines.

Verse 12 of 1 Samuel 7 tells of Samuel's erecting a monument that he called Ebenezer, "for, he said, 'Thus far the LORD has helped us.'" The hymn "Come, Thou Fount of Every Blessing" has a line it that states, "Here I raise mine Ebenezer."[26] This incident is the source of that line. The monument memorialized God's help.

Verses 15-17 of 1 Samuel 7 summarize Samuel's long and praiseworthy career of serving God and the people. All was well. In fact, all was great. But Camelot could not last, for Samuel could not last.

As happens with everyone, Samuel's time was slipping away. A succession plan was needed.

Verses 1-3 of 1 Samuel 8 tell of the problem. Samuel's sons were unworthy to succeed him. Someone new was needed. Maybe more than a new someone was needed. Maybe it was time for the tribes to change their pattern of government.

Here's What We Want (8:4-9)

In 1 Samuel 8:4-5, the elders laid out the problem and their solution. They told Samuel they wanted "a king to govern us," just as the surrounding nations had. They believed they would prosper and be victorious over the surrounding nations if they also had a king just as the surrounding nations did.

Look more closely at what the elders were asking, though. Up to this time, the various tribes were only loosely joined together. There was no central government. Each tribe simply went its own way. They knew they were the same people, and they served and worshiped the same God. However, they acted together only when faced by an outside threat. Most of the time even then, though, only a few tribes might join forces, not all of them. The fancy name for that kind of governmental organization was amphictyony. They were not a united nation but a loose confederation of tribes.

There was a larger problem with the elders' asking for a king. In the time of the judges, here is how things went in the life of Israel. Things would be going well. Then the people would go astray from God and follow other gods. Then God would punish the people by sending "plunderers who plundered them"—enemies (Judges 2:14).

The people would be in great distress and cry out to God for help. Their crying out to God generally meant that they repented of their sins. Then "the Lord would be moved to pity" and raise up a judge to deliver them (Judg. 2:18).

In summary, the steps from sin to deliverance went like this in the Book of Judges and up to this point in 1 Samuel: sin, punishment, repentance, deliverance. Now, though, in the elders' asking for a king, they thought they could skip one of the steps. If they had a powerful king as everybody else did, they could skip the repentance step. Maybe they would no longer need God as much as they thought they did.

In verses 6-9, Samuel talked with God about the people's request. God instructed Samuel and also seems to have soothed Samuel's feelings a bit.

> . . . The LORD said to Samuel, "Listen to the voice of the people in all that they say to you; for they have not rejected you, but they have rejected me from being king over them. Just as they have done to me, from the day I brought them up out of Egypt to this day, forsaking me and serving other gods, so also they are doing to you. Now then, listen to their voice; only—you shall solemnly warn them, and show them the ways of the king who shall reign over them."

God repeated this thought in 1 Samuel 10:19. In that verse, the Lord told the people through Samuel, " . . . Today you have rejected your God, who saves you from all your calamities and your distresses; and you have said, 'No! but set a king over us.'"

Of course, in Israel's history as a monarchy, Israel considered the king as in some ways the representative of God. Some of the psalms are royal psalms, celebrating the king in various ways (see Psalms 2; 18; 20; 21; 45; 72; 89; 101; 110; 132; 144).[27] Some of them likely were used at the coronation of the king, in fact (see Pss. 2; 101; 144).[28] The king was the one whom God had provided to guide the people in God's ways.

Israel was a monarchy. That is, they had one ruler, a king. More than that, however, they were a theocracy, with God as the ruler. As with all human beings, it was hard for some of the kings of Israel to remember that God was the true King even when they mouthed the words. They thus gave lip service to God but served themselves and not God. Samuel would have more to say about this in the next verses.

Are You Sure That's What You Want? If You Get What You Want, You'll Also Get This (8:10-18)

In 1 Samuel 8:10, "Samuel reported all the words of the Lord to the people who were asking him for a king." He then went on to tell the people what would happen when they had a king.

Notice in these verses what would happen. The nation would rely on its military rather than on God (1 Sam. 8:11-12). The king would draft the people's sons and daughters into service in the military and in his domestic service (8:11-13). The king would take "the best of your field and your vineyards and your olive groves and give them to his servants" (8:14, NASB). The king would then take a tenth of the people's produce "and give to his officers and to his servants" (8:15, NASB). The king would take the people's children and the people's animals to work for him. In fact, says verse 17, "you yourselves will become his servants."

The key word in this passage is "take." That's what the king would do, Samuel said. Note how often the word "take" appears in these verses to describe what the king would do. It appears in verses 11, 13, 14, 15, 16, 17. The people thought a king would *give* them security and prosperity. Samuel didn't deny that this might happen. He insisted, though, that they would pay a hefty price for it, for the king would *take, take, take, take, take, take.* Samuel was reminding the people that although the king might give them what they wanted, he would take from them all he wanted.

Deuteronomy 17:14-20 spells out what the king was to be like and what the king was to do and not do. He must not acquire wealth for himself or "many wives for himself" (Deuteronomy 17:17). He was to observe "all the words of this law and these statues, neither exalting himself above other members of the community nor turning aside from the commandment" (Deut.17:19-20). The king who lived and ruled in this way was rare, though. The picture Samuel gave of the king's taking is reflected in the reign of King Solomon in 1 Kings

10—11. Solomon and others of the kings of Israel and Judah simply behaved as the kings of other nations did. Samuel had warned the people that this would happen.

In addition, through Samuel, God was telling the people that a new system of government would not solve Israel's problems, for their problems were spiritual in nature.[29] Even while the king took, took, took, took, took, took, the people would not get what they needed—relationship to God. They would not get the security and happiness that they wanted.

Note in verse 18 what the people would do after they had a king for a while. They would "cry out because of [their] king." In the Book of Judges, they had cried out to God because of their enemies. Now they would cry out to God because of their king.[30]

We Still Want What We Want (8:19-20)

So how did the elders of the people respond to what Samuel told them things were going to be like when they got what they wanted? They in essence said, *Well, everybody else has a king, and we still want one, too.*

The elders didn't say it, but maybe they were thinking, too, something like this: *Samuel is an old man who says he's telling us God's message. Maybe he's wrong. Anyway, we still want that shiny thing called a king.*

You Can Have What You Want, But
(8:21-22)

The Lord had a response to that. The Lord in essence said, *Well, you can have what you want. Getting what you want won't solve your problem, though, and you won't be as happy about it as you think you will be.*

Do you suppose God ever responds to us in this way? We want something. We think we just have to have it. We may even insist that God wants us to have it. We may pray for it. When we get it, we discover that the upkeep and repair on whatever it is is higher than we had planned and that it does not leads us to the result we wanted. We get buyer's remorse. This wise saying about this matter is attributed to St. Teresa of Avila, the sixteenth-century religious leader, mystic, and writer:[31] "There are more tears shed over answered prayers than over unanswered prayers." Wrong wants can be expressed unwisely in prayer, even.

We can be thankful, though, that this passage also provides an example of how God works with the choices we make, even the wrong ones. God did work with Israel and its kings, even the bad ones. For the bad ones, he sent prophets not to pray for them but to challenge them (see Micah 3:1-4; Isaiah 3:14-15). For the good ones, God gave them guidance, strength, and wisdom.

Taking the wrong road, making the wrong choice, need not mean we'll never get back on the right road again. It may mean, though, that the journey will be harder than it needed to be if we had followed the Lord's direction to begin with. So, let us be wise about what we want.

So?

So how can we be wise about what we want? A wise little saying from country folk is this: *If you pick up one end of a stick, remember that you're picking up the other end, too.* The saying is a reminder to consider the consequences of an action. There are consequences to getting our wants satisfied. Some of those consequences may be unintended and may not be good, and Samuel reminded the people of that.

There's an even more important practical lesson from this passage. The passage calls us to do what Israel did not do. They did not evaluate and then check their wants by their commitment to God. Their wanting a king to be like everyone else led them to skip their spiritual practice of turning to God. So the passage calls us to evaluate our wants by our relationship to God. *Will receiving what we want lead us closer to God or further away?* We also do well to add, in accord with the second greatest commandment, *Will receiving what we want be harmful to others?* Being faithful to the Lord thus means thinking not of what I *want* but of what others *need*, not of my good but the public good.

To want is not necessarily bad. Change, sometimes good change, comes from satisfying our wants. Let us be wise about what we want, though, by considering all the consequences as much as we can and, more important, by evaluating our wants by our relationships as

children of God. Let us get our wants in line with
love for God and love for our fellow human beings.

16.

Mark 4:26-34
More Than Meets the Eye

Proper 6 (11): Third Sunday after Pentecost

Our society has something of a fetish about bigness. It is not enough to have a mere bowl game; we must have a *Super* bowl game. It is not enough to be a star as an athlete or an entertainer. Now one must be a *super*star. Even our heroes must be larger than life.

About the most ridiculous thing along these lines is something I observed somewhere on a trip. In the middle of nowhere I came upon a sign that exemplifies our concern for big, spectacular things. The big sign, with boxcar-sized letters, said, "The World's Largest Worm Farm"! I'm sorry I don't recall where it was in case you want to see it for yourself.

We definitely are big on bragging. Does it say something about our values when we realize that we are concerned about the big, the spectacular, and the showy, but Jesus was not? Perhaps we should say that Jesus was not at all troubled by littleness. He was willing to plant a seed and then wait patiently for a magnificent harvest. Jesus' plans did not have to begin with a bang, for he knew he was producing something solid, lasting, and abundant. He was not disheartened by a small response at the beginning. He knew that something was happening that was unseen, and he knew that the results would be more magnificent than could be imagined. Do we need to learn from Jesus about such things?

Jesus' Contemporaries and Bigness

Jesus' contemporaries had much the same problem with bigness that we have. As they watched and evaluated Jesus and his ministry, many of them were disturbed. They thought the Messiah would come in with a bang, right every wrong immediately, and usher in immediately and completely the golden age of what they considered to be God's kingdom.

But that was not what was happening as they observed Jesus. True, some sick people were being healed. True, Jesus was preaching a message that seemed compelling to many people. True, he was attracting great crowds. Look, though, at the kind of people who were coming closest to Jesus—tax collectors, sinners, and fishermen, and not the educated religious people, not the intelligentsia, not the armed revolutionaries whom the Messiah would need if he were to overthrow the despised Romans.

What was going on? What gives with this Jesus who was going about preaching the kingdom of God?

In the midst of discussion and controversy like this, Jesus sat down and told some parables.

These parables served the purpose of interpreting the significance of Jesus' ministry.

Jesus told about a sower who sowed some seeds. The seeds fell on four different types of soil. Some seeds fell on the path. Unable to take root, these seeds were eaten by the birds. Others fell on the rocky soil. These seeds sprouted quickly, but they did not have enough depth of earth to grow. They soon withered and died under the sun's scorching heat. Some seeds fell among the thornbushes. The thornbushes choked them out. But other seeds fell on the good soil. They produced a phenomenally abundant harvest—thirty and sixty and a hundredfold.

What was Jesus saying? He saying that the problem was not with himself and his message of the kingdom. The lack of response lay with the hearers. But listen, he was saying: the harvest will come, and it will be abundant. Would the hearers share in that harvest?

Then Jesus told a parable about a lamp. Jesus' ministry might seem like a lamp that is hidden, but one day it would shine brilliantly to all.

Finally Jesus told the two parables of the Scripture text. The first is about a man who planted seeds. The earth covered the seeds, and from the outside it appeared that nothing was happening. The man got up every day and went to bed every night. The seeds didn't appear to be doing anything during any of that time. Lo and behold, though, one day when the man got up and looked at his field, there was a change. Some green shoots had poked their way through the soil. The seeds had sprouted. How? It had happened automatically, when it appeared nothing was going on. The seeds grew and produced grain. And then the harvest came. It had looked like nothing was happening. It had looked like the sower was derelict in his duty. But something unseen was happening. Under the earth, the seeds were growing toward the harvest.

It looked like nothing was happening in the ministry of Jesus, too, as many, especially the religious leaders, saw it. But something was happening indeed in Jesus' ministry, and it would grow to fulfillment. That was certain.

The second parable has to do with a very small object, a mustard seed. You would see it, and you would say, there's nothing to that. That will never amount to anything.

The Jews considered the mustard seed to be the smallest of all seeds. What happens when the mustard seed is sown, though? It grows up and becomes the greatest of all shrubs. It makes large branches. Birds make their nests in its shade. Isn't that a surprise when you realize it all began with a tiny seed?

The harvest of Jesus' ministry and message would be just as surprising, even more surprising, to some. What Jesus was doing seemed so small and insignificant. How could anything ever come of that? So people questioned. But the harvest would be abundant. The kingdom of God was present and in action in the ministry of Jesus, although it did not seem so to some. The harvest of this kingdom would be openly apparent later. Many would come to find shelter in its branches. What a contrast between the small beginning and the magnificent result!

Toward Personal Meaning

Look at these truths in terms of personal meaning for our lies. Could there be more than meets the eye in the ministry of Jesus among us still?

What about the first parable, the parable about the seed growing automatically toward the harvest when it seemed nothing was happening? The sower had sown the seeds. He had done what he could. Therefore, let him rest in the faith and hope that the harvest would come. Could there be a message here for us? Don't we often get impatient, thinking that nothing is happening with the seeds we have sown?

A wise observer of human life said a few years that civilization's three major killers are not heart disease, cancer, and accidents. Instead, they are calendars, clocks, and telephones. These devices are representative of the pressures of life. They are representative, too, of our desire to do it all ourselves, unmindful of the faith that we have a Heavenly Father who cares for us eternally. This parable calls us back to this faith and to the hope of what God will certainly do for those who trust in him.

When the sower had sown the seeds to the best of his ability, then he must trust patiently in the activity that was going on underneath the soil. Do we? Or are we constantly digging up the seeds and dusting them off to see whether anything is happening yet?

It was difficult for the disciples to rest in hope in this manner. The next incident after the parables has the disciples and Jesus journeying across the Sea of Galilee in a boat. Jesus was asleep. A great storm of wind arose, and waves washed over and into the boat. The disciples could not rest, however, even though the Son of God was in the boat with them.

Jesus himself was the prime example of faith and hope, waiting in confidence for the seed to sprout and the harvest to come. Think a minute. How would you have handled life if you had been Jesus, with the terrific responsibility God had placed on him and with the knowledge of the great need of humankind? Most likely, we would have been frantic, running here and there, engaged in endless activity. But Jesus could sleep. Jesus could rest. Jesus could wait patiently for the seed to sprout. He trusted in God. He believed the harvest of his work and ministry was certain.

Such an approach is surely the secret of his life and ministry. Helmut Thielicke, the great German preacher, talked about this aspect of Jesus' life and character. He asked,

> Why was it that he spoke with authority, as the scribes and Pharisees did not? . . . He spoke with such power because he had first spoken with the Father, because always he came out of silence. He rested in eternity and therefore broke into time with

such power. That's why he is so disturbing to time. He lived in communion with God. . . .[32]

On the other hand, we become involved in endless activity. We neglect the resource of prayer and communion with God. We seek to do and perform and act, often simply in order to please other people. We neglect to get our lives in line with God and God's power. We become troubled, burdened, worried, and anxious. We are unwilling to believe we may in faith rest in the hope of what God will do.

As the bit of doggerel has it, "When in trouble, when in doubt, run in circles, scream and shout." We see and hear that a lot these days, certainly among political leaders but even among church leaders, not to mention the shrill comments we see on social media. Every little thing is the worst crisis since the world began, and anyone who doesn't agree with the speaker is obviously out of touch and worse.

This is not to say that we should do nothing or that some things do not deserve strong words and strong action. After all, the sower labored to sow the seed. There is a place for effort and action, and there is a place for trusting God while we are doing so and as we await the harvest.

What about the second parable, the parable about the mustard seed that became a huge tree? This parable contrasts the small beginning with the magnificent result. Jesus was saying that something was going to happen that was far beyond what was visible at the time and far beyond the expectations of the people who heard him, especially the religious leaders.

For us, too, there is more than meets the eye that will happen. The small seed will make a great tree.

It is hard to remember and live by this truth. Sometimes we come to the end of the day or the week or the month or maybe even a lifetime, and we have a sense of discouragement. Maybe we have done our best. We have sought to do the Father's will. We wonder why the lack of results. What do we have to show for our work?

Sometimes we feel this way about the church's work. What do we have to show for our efforts? It is easy to forget that the mustard seed becomes the greatest of all shrubs. It is easy to forget that the church serves as a leaven in society, often working quietly, lovingly, and patiently in the character and decisions of individuals. It is easy to forget that the character of children, of young people, of adults is being molded, and that impulses to right living are being translated into action.

Of course, we cannot help but be aware of how poorly Christians sometimes behave, and we cannot help but remember that we do not always do our best, either as individuals or as a church. But still by the grace of God the seed is being sown, and the mustard seed is producing the greatest of all shrubs. Results are being brought forth by the grace of God.

Reuel Howe, a preacher and writer, tells about an incident from his childhood that illustrates such a hope. He and his parents lived a long distance from any neighbors. One day their house caught fire and burned to the ground. They lost everything except the clothes on their backs. He and his father walked to the closest village to buy supplies in order to live and begin again.

When they returned, they found an unusual sight. His mother had somehow found some food, prepared lunch, reclaimed a few eating utensils, and placed all of it on a log. In the middle of all of this, she had put a rusty tin can filled with wildflowers.

For the child, that rusty tin can filled with flowers meant hope, that it was not all over, that they could go on from there. Maybe they had only a mustard seed of hope, but that was enough to begin with. All three of them gathered around that tin can full of flowers believed the family would make it, and they did.[33]

We will, too. There's more than meets the eye about us and about what God has done, is doing, and will do.

17.

1 Samuel 17:57—18:16
Facing the Green-Eyed Monster

Proper 7 (12): Fourth Sunday after Pentecost

When you saw or heard the title of this
meditation, perhaps you immediately recalled its
source. Of course, the image is part of our culture,
but I confess that I had to search for its source
when I thought of it. It comes, as do so many of
our picturesque expressions in the English
language, from Shakespeare. His play *Othello* is
more than 400 years old, but it's right on target in
how it deals with our besetting sin of jealousy, or
envy. In the play, Shakespeare puts these words
into the mind and mouth of Iago, the villain of the
story. Motivated by deceit, Iago says to Othello,

> O, beware, my lord, of jealousy;
> It is the green-eyed monster which doth
> mock
> The meat it feeds on . . . .[34]

Iago is using these words about jealousy to
lead Othello astray, but they are still true and
instructive. Jealousy is indeed a monster that
destroys. In the play, jealousy destroys lives. It
destroys the life of Othello and the life of
Desdemona his wife, and it wreaks havoc on other

163

lives. At the end of the play, Othello kills his wife, thinking she has committed adultery, and then kills himself when he finds out that she hasn't. The play is one of Shakespeare's great studies of human nature and the messes and tragedies in which we human beings often involve ourselves.

Since jealousy is a close synonym of envy, we can think of it as one of the classic seven deadly sins. Thomas Aquinas passed along to us from s seventh-century scholar of the church, Saint John of Damascus, this definition of envy: "sorrow for another's good."[35] In other words, jealousy or envy is our response of sadness when something good happens to someone else.

The novelist and preacher Frederick Buechner also has a picturesque description of envy. He describes envy this way: "Envy is the consuming desire to have everybody else be as unsuccessful as you are."

So where do we see envy or jealousy these days? At least three places stand out—sibling rivalry, romantic relationships, and work relationships. Interestingly, Othello's problem with envy began in a work relationship. Iago felt Othello should have promoted him instead of someone else, and Iago spent the rest of the play getting even. He did it by using a romantic relationship, the relationship of Othello to his wife Desdemona.

And sibling rivalry? That is not limited to children. Unresolved sibling rivalry often comes out when the parents pass on and the will is read.

Envy or jealousy happens elsewhere. It even happens in business. Jim Collins is a highly successful business management consultant. One of the observations he makes in his best-selling books, which include *Built to Last* and *Good to Great*, is that comparison is America's corporate sin. That is, a corporation looks around at the success of another corporation and decides to try to emulate it rather than to do what it can do best. That's pretty close to jealousy and envy, isn't it?

King Saul and Jealousy

In this passage of Scripture, King Saul of Israel provides a powerful example of jealousy. He felt insecure about himself and his abilities, and so he let himself become jealous of a person with obviously greater abilities.

Actually, Saul had good reason to feel insecure. Perhaps you recall the old joke about the troubled fellow who went to a psychiatrist for help. The psychiatrist asked him, *What seems to be the problem?* He replied, *I think I have an inferiority complex.* After a few visits, the psychiatrist told him, *Well, relax, you don't have an inferiority complex. You're just inferior.*

Saul was the first king of Israel, the only king Israel had ever had. Saul had fouled up, big time, more than once. He had started out being a humble fellow who questioned why he should be king (1 Samuel 9:21). He ended up as a person who believed he deserved every bit of power he had and more. He took power that didn't belong to him (1 Sam. 13:8-15; 15:17-21). As a result, the prophet Samuel had already told Saul that his kingship would not endure (13:14; 15:23).

So, it is no wonder that Saul felt insecure. He became a scheming person. Toward the end of his life, long after this incident in 1 Samuel 18, he became a pitiable figure, beset by doubts and depression. These incidents in 1 Samuel 18 provide a view of Saul's life that shows part of how Saul sank lower and lower.

Introducing David (17:57—18:5)

This passage provides one picture of how David became part of Saul's inner circle. After David had taken care of the Philistine giant Goliath, Abner brought David to Saul. Abner was the leader of Saul's army.

Things moved swiftly after David's arrival. For some reason, Jonathan, the son of the king, took an immediate liking to David. As the text puts it, " . . . The soul of Jonathan was bound to the soul of David, and Jonathan loved him as his own soul" (18:1). The word translated "soul" here refers to one's inner being. Jonathan and David became fast friends.

Verses 3-4 show the extent to which Jonathan went to solidify his friendship with David. "Jonathan made a covenant with David . . ." (18:4). To demonstrate that covenant, Jonathan gave him his princely robe and even his armor (18:5). We assume that David entered into this covenant with the same level of commitment Jonathan did, but we are not told.

166

Jonathan's daddy, King Saul, also took an immediate liking to David. We are not told precisely why. Perhaps it was because David had charisma, which he likely did. Perhaps Saul was appreciative of David's victory over the Philistines by killing Goliath. Perhaps Saul saw great potential in David for the nation. Perhaps Saul saw David as a way to shore up his own faltering kingship. Whatever the reason, the king wouldn't "let him return to his father's house" (18:2). David became part of the royal court.

Saul also sent David out on missions for him and even put him over the army. David was always successful in his assignments.

So, everybody liked David. The people liked David. Saul's servants liked David. To this point, evidently even Saul liked David. All might have been well, or at least better, if Saul had been able to keep doing that. If Saul had continued to revel in the success of his gifted young subordinate, everybody might well have liked Saul, too. After all, Saul had found David, brought him into his kingly court, and encouraged David in his success. But Saul wasn't up to the task of reveling in anyone else's success, whether for the good of the nation or the good of himself. Everything about Saul was *me, me, me.*

Sad About Another's Success (18:6-9)

Things came to a head with Saul when Saul heard about a great celebration and found that he wasn't the center of it. All the women of Israel were singing and dancing, but not for him. Oh, they were giving him praise. In fact, Saul

167

certainly would have liked the first stanza of the song, "Saul has slain his thousands" (18:7). But then Saul heard that next stanza: "And David his ten thousands" (18:7).

Then they sang it again. And again. And again. That song became number one in the nation that day, and Saul couldn't get it out of his head. It was somewhat like your hearing some song in a television or radio commercial. You don't like it. It grates on your last nerve. But you just can't stop hearing it in your head even though you can't stand it.

Saul went further than hearing the song, of course. He began to think about the meaning of the song. The people weren't singing that song about him. In addition, the song meant David was no longer Saul's protégé. The people could have praised Saul for having a protégé like David. But Saul began to see David as not a protégé but a rival and a threat. So Saul asked himself, " . . . What more can he have but the kingdom?" (18:8). As far as Saul was concerned, there was no answer to that rhetorical question, and it disturbed him greatly.

So Saul "looked at David with suspicion from that day on" (18:9). The literal Hebrew is something like *Saul eyed David with his eye* from then on. There's a bluegrass song that tells a sad story about some suspicious goings-on. It has this line it: "I'm going to sleep with one eye open from now on."[36] That was Saul in his jealousy about David.

Jealousy in Action (18:10-16)

Right soon, "the next day," in fact, Saul began to take action on his jealousy (18:10). The text seems to suggest that God was behind this action. "An evil spirit from God came mightily upon Saul" (18:10). In looking at this text, we must see it in the context of beliefs in that day rather than our own. In that day, as Israel was growing and learning about pretty much everything, including God, there was no idea at all about secondary causation. If something happened, God did it. God caused everything directly.

In light of the thought of that day, then, we would understand this passage better if we saw it as either an instance of Saul's verging toward insanity or of Saul's letting himself act in a fully self-centered and thus sinful way. Later on he would become so angry at his son Jonathan that he would even try to kill him (20:33). Either diagnosis—insanity or sinful self-centeredness— would fit such an act. Perhaps it was a bit of both. Whatever the case, this incident with David was the beginning of Saul's slide into a jealous rage so extreme that he attempted to murder David and later even Jonathan.

Saul did remove David "from his presence" (18:13). But then he promoted David to "his commander of a thousand" (18:13). He even gave one of his daughters to David in marriage. So Saul gave David a promotion and a marriage. Why would Saul do such things? It looks like the marriage was cover for a plan to eventually get rid of David without alarming the people. After all, "all Israel and Judah loved David" (18:16). Even a king of Israel needed political support from the people.

What Saul wanted eventually to happen with David is told in verse 17. He wanted the Philistines to kill David in battle.

So?

So what does this passage teach us? Here are a few thoughts: (1) Jealousy is a very powerful feeling. (2) Jealousy can lead to tragic consequences. (3) If we look at our lives as God looks at them, there's no need to be jealous.

There's an old story that goes back to the days when international travel was much more common by ship than by airplane. A missionary couple was returning home after a lifetime of service. Traveling on the same ship was a world-famous celebrity. When the ship docked, a huge crowd was waiting and cheering. They were waiting and cheering for the celebrity, though, not for the returning missionaries. The missionary husband turned to his wife and said, dejectedly, *We are returning home, but no one is here to meet us and cheer for us.* She said to him, *But dear, we're not home yet.*

Whether that story actually happened, I don't know. I know this one did, though. Bert and Ruth Dyson were a missionary couple I once knew. We were in church with them in Nashville. They were gifted, educated, caring, generous, competent, good people. My hunch is they would have been successful, perhaps even monetarily, wherever and however they chose to spend their lives. But they followed God's call to be missionaries.

For health reasons, Bert and Ruth came back from Sierra Leone to retire. They had served in Nigeria before that. They had very few worldly possessions. They had no house, no land, probably little money, only a monthly pension. They lived in the missionary residence our church provided. Ruth once pointed to thirteen trunks that had just arrived. They had been shipped from Africa to our church's missionary residence. Ruth said about them, "Those are all our worldly possessions." Neither she nor Burt seemed to be jealous of those who had more, though.

How could that be? As missionaries, Bert and Ruth had invested their lives in people, giving of themselves without reserve. Friends of mine who visited the couple both in Nigeria and in Sierra Leone, said unanimously, *You cannot imagine how revered Bert and Ruth are among the people where they lived and worked. Everywhere we went the people spoke in tones of reverence, respect, and gratitude for them. You cannot imagine the impact of their lives on the people they served.*

Another friend who had visited them in Nigeria reported that the people referred to Bert as the "big man" because of the greatness of his contributions. Quite a legacy, with no jealousy about not having accumulated wealth as others had done.[37]

As we continue to think about jealousy, consider another thought. James Mulholland, a theologian, pastor, and author, tells how as a teenager he was jealous of his brother. He was jealous because his father had bought his brother a motorcycle. The gift was very extravagant, and the teenage James Mulholland was incensed. Reflecting years later, he wrote,

> I was jealous of my father's apparent favoritism. When I complained to my father, he pulled me aside, and said, "Your brother is having a difficult time right now. I needed to give him that motorcycle as a sign of my love. I need you to trust that I love you as much as I love him."[38]

Sometimes when we are tempted to be jealous, we should take a step back and ask whether we have all the facts about the situation.

How can we avoid jealousy? We can do it mainly by being secure in ourselves, in who we are, but more than that in what God empowers and calls us to be and do. We do it also by recognizing that worldly status and seeming worldly success are not the best gauges of status and success. We do it also by not jumping to conclusions, as King Saul did, as James Mulholland did, and as lots of other people still do.

As Iago advised Othello, let us

> beware . . . of jealousy;
> It is the green-eyed monster . . . .

The green-eyed monster of jealousy mocks us and leads us to disaster if we do not avoid it or reject it.

18.

Mark 5:21-43
Victory in Jesus?

Proper 8 (13): Fifth Sunday after Pentecost

How do you respond to the two stories in this text and others like them in the Bible? There's a good chance we have more than one response.

Perhaps we find ourselves unwilling to doubt them, for we know what it is to need help and to need it badly. We know that in many situations in life we have no one to turn to but God. For own benefit, we want very much to believe that these two stories are true and that they can be true for us in our situations of dire need.

But we also may find it difficult to believe them. They have about them the marks of dreams and wishes, and not reality. A woman is healed from an incurable illness that had disrupted her life for twelve years. A child is restored to life, brought back from the sleep of death.

Perhaps we think, *How wonderful!* At the same time we think, *How unbelievable!* We live in a world where storms come and we are frightened, where people get sick and don't get well, where loved ones die and we can only stand by feeling helpless and hopeless, wanting to hold back death but unable to. Because of who we are as people who believe the Bible, we likely are unwilling to doubt that there is victory in Jesus, but we may well be unable to believe that it can really be true for us.

As we look at this passage, let us bring our experiences of need and loss and lay them side by side with the Scriptures. Let us think about two questions concerning this matter of victory in Jesus, the victory that Jairus and his wife and little daughter experienced and the victory that the woman with the issue of blood felt in her body.

First, is there victory in Jesus?

Second, if there is, how can I experience this victory in my life for my deep needs and the needs of people I love?

Is There Victory in Jesus?

Is there really victory in Jesus? Is Jesus' power sufficient to snatch victory out of defeat, to save us and our loved ones from illness, death, or whatever tragedy in which we may be caught?

The biblical evidence is certain and clear. Yes, there is victory in Jesus.

That's what we see in this entire section of Scripture in the Gospel of Mark. Earlier the disciples and Jesus had been out in a boat on the Sea of Galilee. Jesus was asleep. A great storm arose. The disciples were terrified. Greatly disturbed, they awakened Jesus. He rebuked the wind and said to the waves, in effect, *Quiet! Be still!* And it was so. There was victory in Jesus.

174

Then Jesus had met the man who lived among the tombs. The man was beside himself, disturbed—possessed by an unclean spirit, the Scripture says. He was so split inside himself that he was many selves and not just one. He could not get himself together to live in integrity as one whole person. Then Jesus came. Jesus rid the man of the demons and made him whole again. When the frightened people from the area arrived, there was the man, sitting, clothed, and in his right mind. There was victory in Jesus.

Then came Jairus, a ruler of the synagogue. As any parent would have been, he was at his wit's end. Any sensitive parent can hear the anguish in Jairus's voice. Perhaps we have voiced such anguish ourselves. Few things tear at a parent's heart than his or her child who is sick or in some other trouble—no matter how old or young the child is, whether the child is four or forty, and no matter what the trouble is. This father's heart was breaking within him. Jairus begged Jesus, "My little daughter is at the point of death. Come and lay your hands on her, so that she may be made well and live" (Mark 5:23).

On the way, another person needed Jesus. A woman, ill for twelve years, sought Jesus' help. Here again there was anguish and heartbreak. Her difficulty was not just an inconvenience. Her hemorrhaging would have meant that people shunned her. She was unclean—unacceptable, an outcast. She had tried to get well, but she just couldn't. The doctors hadn't helped her. She had spent all she had trying to get well. But now she was worse, not better. She, too, was at her wit's end. Only someone who has been there or who has been close to someone else who has been there can understand the depth of her anguish.

Then Jesus came. The woman was too embarrassed to approach Jesus directly and state her problem, evidently. So she said to herself, "If I but touch his clothes, I will be made well" (5:28). That's what she did, and she was healed. Surely it was an error to treat Jesus' garments as having some magical power. I tell you, though, people have a hard time paying much attention to settling theological debates when they are desperately ill. They just want to get well, however it can happen. The fact is that God honored her faith. She did not understand it all, but God honored her faith. There was victory in Jesus.

What about Jairus's daughter, sick to the point of death? Would there be victory in Jesus for her? Messengers came saying she was already dead. But Jesus said to Jairus, "Do not fear, only believe" (5:36).

At the home, the professional mourners were already about their gruesome business, yelling and screaming. For them, maybe it was just another job, just another funeral. But what's that this Jesus was saying? "The child is not dead but sleeping" (5:39). That's a laugh. Who does Jesus think he is, anyway? God?

But inside, Jesus took the child's hand and said, *Little darling, it's time to get up*. And she did. She was alive! There is victory in Jesus.

Over and over, before and after these events, there were healings and other miraculous happenings. Lepers were cleansed, blind people were made to see, deaf people were made to hear, disturbed people were made whole, hungry people were fed. Divine mercy acted in Jesus to overcome human desperation. There was victory in Jesus.

So the old, old story tells us, and we at least partly believe it. How we want to believe it. How we need to believe it.

But, of course, there is a problem—at least two or three really. First, Jesus didn't heal every single person then. There was still sickness and death in the world. Second, even the little girl eventually died, although it might have been years and years later. Death finally comes to us all.

Perhaps more personal to us, when our own needs have been desperate, we have asked, begged, and pleaded, but Jesus does not seem to us to have come to help. We and our loved ones haven't been healed. We have had to stand by open graves. The storm has come, and the winds and waves have brought destruction. We have not been delivered.

So we may have a hard time saying there is victory in Jesus. Oh, yes, it might have happened in the Bible. But why hasn't it happened for me? What we really want to know is whether there is victory in Jesus now, for us. We do not want to say, *No.* How can we say, *Yes?*

It may see to be a cop-out to say that our ways are not God's ways. It may seem we are sentimentally evading the question. But maybe it's not.

The fact is that our ideas about what is good and bad and best and worst may need some rearranging. Our ways really are not God's ways. As Helmut Thielicke, the great German preacher and theologian, put it:

> One day, perhaps, when we look back from God's throne on the last day we shall say with amazement and surprise, "If I had ever dreamed when I stood at the graves of my loved ones and everything seemed to be ended; . . . if I had ever dreamed when I faced the meaningless fate of an endless imprisonment or a malignant disease; if I had ever dreamed that God was only carrying out his design and plan through all these woes, that in the midst of my cares and troubles and despair *his* harvest was ripening . . . if I had known this I would have been more calm and confident; yes, then I would have been more cheerful and far more tranquil and composed.[39]

Now, there is something about that statement that is helpful, and there is something about it I resist. I cannot feel right in thinking that God sends evil on us, especially not on little children. But perhaps there is some truth in what the preacher was saying, that our ways are not God's ways and that if we had insight into the mind of God we might think differently about the circumstances that befall us. Perhaps that would help us to see there is truly victory in Jesus in spite of our human difficulties in understanding.

We may need to see even the mysterious, terrible figure of death from a new perspective. Perhaps we need to see it not as an end but as a passageway, by God's grace. The African-American poet, James Weldon Johnson, has a poem called "Go Down Death" that expresses this.[40] It is written out of the author's memory of the sermons of old black preachers. The poem begins,

> And God said: Go down, Death, go down,
> Go down to Savannah, Georgia,
> Down in Yamacraw,
> And find Sister Caroline.
> She's born the burden and heat of the day,
> She's labored long in my vineyard,
> And she's tired—
> She's weary.
> Go down, Death, and bring her to me. . . .
>
> While we were watching round her bed,
> She turned her eyes and looked away,
> She saw what we couldn't see:
> She saw Old Death. She saw Old Death
> Coming like a falling star.
> But death didn't frighten Sister Caroline:
> He looked to her like a welcome friend.
> And she whispered to us: I'm ging home,
> And she smiled and closed her eyes. . . .
>
> Weep not, weep not,
> She is not dead;
> She's resting in the bosom of Jesus.

Would it help us to see more victory in Jesus if we changed our perspective, too? At least it might help if we could indeed know that our ways are not God's ways.

Along with this we may say that sometimes we must wait longer for God's victory than we wish. We want it now; we may have to wait.

But we need to know that always there is victory. Sometimes God delivers us fully, miraculously it seems. We do get well. Thanks to doctors and medicine or perhaps to what, humanly speaking, we do not know, we get well. Sometimes God does deliver us, fully and miraculously.

Sometimes God delivers, but not as we had hoped. A minister tells of a dynamic Christian woman in Brazil. She had been a beautiful, gifted pianist for a concert orchestra. She had been awarded a scholarship to study music in Europe. But something happened. She contracted leprosy—Hansen's disease. She had to be confined to a leper colony. The disease was arrested, but not before it had taken some of her physical beauty plus her skill as a pianist. In spite of this, she said, "I thank God I became a leper!" Why would she say such a thing? Because through that experience she found God. She said, "To know Christ as my Saviour and Lord is worth all I have suffered, so I thank God I became a leper."[41]

So, is there victory in Jesus? Yes!

How Can We Experience Victory in Jesus?

How can we experience this victory for ourselves? How can we put this feeble faith of ours to work so that we can experience victory in Jesus?

First, let your purpose be God's purpose. We must do better than to treat God as Santa Claus and expect indulgence for our whims. We must seek to let our purpose be God's purpose.

Likely to do that we will have to change our purpose. We may have to acknowledge that we do not know what is best, that our ideas about what is best may even be wrong, way wrong. Because our ways are not God's ways and our time is not God's time, we must acknowledge that our purpose may need to be changed. Jesus prayed that he might escape the cross, but he also prayed that God's will be done. He was willing to bring his purpose in line with God's purpose.

Second, find out what you need. When you have placed God's will above your own and have sought as best you can to seek God's will, then try to focus on what you believe God's will is, what it is that you need done. Jairus knew what he needed. He needed his little daughter to be brought back from death's door. The woman with the issue of blood knew her need, too. Twelve long agonizing years she had existed with this condition in her body. She needed to be made well.

The woman knew what she needed, and Jairus knew, too. Do we? Do you know what you need? Many things do not come to us because we do not want them badly enough. We say we want a better life. How badly do we want it?

Third, surrender yourself and your need to Jesus. It is amazing that both Jairus and the woman did not feel hopeless about their situations. Maybe they thought Jesus was their last hope, but they still had hope. So they were able to come in surrender. They came and laid their case before Jesus. In the woman's case, she had surrendered to the point that she believed that even a touch of Jesus' garment would bring her victory. In Jairus's case, he believed in spite of the ridicule he received. Jesus had told Jairus, "Do not fear, only believe" (5:36), and that is what Jairus had done.

Are you willing to surrender all you are, have, and hope to be to Jesus, to cast your all on him? Then you can know victory in Jesus.

Fourth, surrender again. Frankly, it is tough to surrender, truly surrender. Both Jairus and the woman had to cross high and strong barriers to truly surrender.

Even so, in spite of all that comes against us, there can be victory in Jesus. When the doctor says, *We have done all we can, and the rest is in God' hands,* even then there can be victory in Jesus.

It may seem to be too simple, too unbelievable, but these are the words we need to hear, believe, and live by: "Do not fear, only believe."

19.

Mark 6:1-13
A Pattern for Christian Living

Proper 9 (14): Sixth Sunday after Pentecost

A person who became an influential Christian leader tells about a mistake he made when he was a college student. One summer during his college days, he worked for his uncle, who built houses. His uncle assigned him the task of cutting some boards, all the same length. There were thousands of boards to be cut, for his uncle was building many houses during those days. His uncle left him with a board that was cut the exact length desired. The student was to use this board as a pattern. But instead of using the board as a pattern, he began simply to use the last board he had cut as a pattern for the next one.[42]

Perhaps you can guess what happened. If you perhaps can't, don't do what he did. He cut hundreds of boards that day, following that pattern. He would cut one board and then use that board to cut the next one. He did this over and over.

Later that day, his uncle came back to see how his college-boy nephew was doing. The uncle, an experienced carpenter and builder, saw the problem immediately, and it probably was a good thing the college student was a relative whom the patient uncle evidently liked.

The young man's uncle had him compare the length of the boards he had cut. The boards he had cut later in the day were as much as six inches longer than the board he had started out with and was supposed to have used as a pattern. His uncle taught him a fundamental rule of carpentry that day—the importance of using the right measuring stick.

That's a principle for life, too, including for the Christian life. This passage of Scripture can provide us with some guidance for a pattern for Christian living—a sort of measuring stick that can help us toward true Christian living.

Like you, I cringe sometimes at the ways the word "Christian" is used and at the attempts, some of them well-meaning, to develop a rigid definition for who is and who isn't a Christian. But consider how Jesus' sending out of the disciples in Mark 6:7-13 might help us toward a healthy pattern by which to measure our lives.

Jesus had just faced the unbelief of those who had known him while he was growing up, and Mark 6:1-6 serves as a reminder of the challenges Jesus and his disciples would face as Jesus continued his mission. Even so, Jesus' sending out the disciples provided a pattern they were to follow in spite of any difficulty they might face in this mission.

Sent Out on Jesus' Mission

The Twelve had already been with Jesus for some time now. They had observed what he did, and they had learned from him. Now Jesus sent them out on a mission—his mission.

As we continue to consider the Gospel of Mark, we will see that the disciples were far from understanding Jesus completely. In fact, even after they had traveled with Jesus and learned from him, they definitely did not understand him. But yet they obeyed him. When he called the Twelve, they came. When he sent them out, they went. They did not understand Jesus or even believe in him as fully as they needed to, but they obeyed him when he called and commanded them.

Don't we often do it in just the opposite way? We may claim our faith is strong, that we believe in Christ, that we understand who he is. But do we obey him? Do we come when he calls and go out when he sends? The disciples were obedient even though their faith was weak. We often are disobedient even though we claim to believe and to believe strongly.

Jesus sent the Twelve, and they were obedient to that sending. We, though, can be specialists in excuse-finding and barrier-building. We say, *I know that's what the Lord said, but here's what I think he really meant for our day.* Or we say, *I know that's what the Lord said, but just this once won't hurt.* Or, *I know that's what the Lord said, but I really want this person or these people to like me, so. . . .*

How often have I talked to people who have slipped away from the Christian life through just such things—acts of unfaithfulness, little indiscretions, which perhaps they considered small and in which they saw little harm.

All of us have likely had some experience with these little things we call viruses that get blamed for so much. All of us have suffered the misery that "having a virus" can cause. Someone has calculated that it would take a half-million viruses laid end to end to make a line as long as the word *virus* on a printed page in ordinary-sized type. But what damage they cause us, all the way from the merely irritating to the deadly. Just so do our supposedly little acts of unfaithfulness hurt our truly living the Christian life.

But more than simply inward obedience is at stake in this passage of Scripture. Jesus was sending the Twelve out on a mission to the people around them. He was giving them the responsibility of helping him arouse the people to their need to turn to God.

Such a mission is part of our obedience, too. We are sent, too, on a mission for Christ—to care for and minister to all people, but especially to those often spoken of as *the last, the least, and the lost*—the people whom society has put at the back of the line or otherwise disregarded and even condemned, and the people, the up-and-in as well as the down-and-out, who are on the wrong track in life.

Empowered for Service

The Twelve were not expected to serve Jesus on their own, in their own strength, and alone. Neither are we. They were empowered for service, and so are we.

As Jesus sent out the disciples, he gave them "authority." Already they had been with Jesus and had surely been strengthened inwardly through their contact with him. Jesus was now sending them out as his personal representatives. He also gave them "authority" as they went out. He empowered them for service.

Recall who these disciples were. They had been frightened in a storm on the Sea of Galilee. Later, after this passage of Scripture, even after they had seen Jesus feed a multitude of people not just once but twice, they did not understand. But when Jesus sent them out empowered for service, they went.

As we seek to live the Christian life, let us beware of saying, *I can't*, when we feel nudged toward some act of Christian service. Where there is an awareness of need and a willingness to meet it, we can count on God to supply the power and the resources. Let us not say *no* when God's power would enable us to say *yes*. On the other hand, let us not say *yes* and think we can do it on our own. Let us be open to being empowered by God.

Instructed by Jesus

Jesus instructed the Twelve for their mission. The instructions likely seem unusual to us, but they were purposeful.

Jesus told them "to take nothing for their journey except a staff; no bread, no bag, no money in their belts; but to wear sandals and to put on two tunics" (Mark 5:8-9). That is, they were to take only the minimum for the journey—the traveler's staff and sandals; only one small carry-on, no checked bags. They were to depend on the Lord and the hospitality of others for their provisions of food and shelter. They were not to carry a beggar's bag with the thought of financial reward.

They were to depend on the Lord and be satisfied with the hospitality people extended them. They were to remain in the house that accepted them and not be looking around for better quarters.

They were on important business, God's business. If they and their message were rejected, the affront was not simply to them but to the Lord. If they and their message were not accepted, they were simply to move on to a more receptive place.

In short, Jesus instructed the disciples to depend on God, for they were on God's business, not their own. They were to go in dependence on God. They were to live disciplined lives.

Are there instructions here for us? Are we willing to depend on God rather than being concerned abut the almighty dollar and the pressure of public opinion? Are we willing to see the supreme importance of God's work? Are we willing to be disciplined in our living so that we might carry out that work with the commitment it deserves?

Faithful to Responsibilities

Verse 12 notes, "So they went out and proclaimed that all should repent. They cast out many demons, and anointed with oil many who were sick and cured them." They simply did what they were told. They didn't just talk about what they were going to do or what they ought to do. They just did it. They were faithful to the responsibilities Jesus had given them.

That is our call, too—to be faithful. Nowhere are we called to be successful, but faithfulness is demanded.

Perhaps the one question we ought to ask ourselves at the end of the day or at the end of some task is this: *Did you do your best?* To know that we have done our best is the standard toward which we ought to strive. It gives us a high standard, but it also frees us from false standards. If we have done our best and the response has not been what it should have been, we can still take heart. The call is to be faithful. A well-known musician said, "I love my music. Somebody else might do better. I couldn't, so I'm happy." Another said, "It is a wonderful satisfaction to me to be able to say, 'I couldn't do any better.'"

Could you say that of yourself? Have you done your best? Why not? That is the call that comes to us. We are to be faithful.

Successful?

The disciples were sent out on Jesus' mission, empowered for service, instructed in how to do it, and faithful in their responsibilities. Were they successful? Their very faithfulness made them successful. But there evidently was outward success, too. Earlier in the Gospel of Mark, Jesus told a parable that indicated that although all the response to his ministry would not be positive, an abundant harvest was certain. Many would not listen. There would be many failures. But many would "hear the word and accept it and bear fruit, thirty and sixty and a hundredfold" (4:20).

When we follow the pattern of Christian living described in Jesus' sending out the disciples, there will be success. It may not be spectacular, showy, and overwhelming. There may be many failures and difficulties along the way. Success may not be immediate but on the other side of the cross. Even so, this pattern of life is the only one worth following. We waste our resources and those of others when we do not do that. Recall the college student when he used the wrong pattern for cutting the lumber. I commend Jesus' pattern for Christian living to you.

20.

2 Corinthians 12:1-10
Your Greatest Strength

Proper 9 (14): Sixth Sunday after Pentecost

"Whenever I am weak, then I am strong," Paul said (2 Corinthians 12:10). The Bible sometimes seems to set before us impossibilities, contradictions, and paradoxes. The truths of the Bible certainly do cut straight across the grain of many of the fondest ideas of our world. This word that Paul sets before us in this text fits in this category.

"Whenever I am weak, then I am strong" (2 Cor. 12:10). This combination of ideas clashes in our minds, at least it does in mine. One part of that sentence seems in direct conflict with the other. It's at least a paradox—two thoughts that appear to contradict each other and yet each is true.

How can we be both weak and strong at the same time? How can strength arise out of weakness?

We are not simply dealing with clever words when we say, "Whenever I am weak, then I am strong" (12:10). Rather we are dealing with a cardinal principle of life. This principle of strength through weakness is firmly embedded in the Christian way, and yet we do have a hard time grasping and learning it.

The truth is, though, that our greatest strength is not in our strength, not at all. Our greatest strength is in our weakness. Our failures, our challenges, and even our defeats and what we do with them often have more to do with whether we will live the abundant life than do our successes.

Still we wonder how this can be so. Let's look at this experience of Paul to see how it can be so and, more, how it can be so for us today.

To me, this Scripture sets forth three foundation stones for this remarkable statement that seems so contradictory in itself and even so out of touch with life. Before we look at these three foundation stones, though, let's refresh our minds about this experience of Paul's to see the background of how they brought strength in his life.

Paul's Experience

This letter we call 2 Corinthians finds Paul in conflict with one of his churches. The church at Corinth was departing from Paul's leadership and setting up their own. They were engaging in practices and believing things that Paul felt to be wrong. They complained about Paul, saying, "His letters are weighty and strong, but his bodily presence is weak, and his speech contemptible" (10:10). These charges were quite serious and personal in nature, and they must have been hard for Paul to hear. He chose to combat them, though, not on the basis of his strengths but his weaknesses.

Paul was doing this as he talked about his mysterious "thorn . . . in the flesh" (12:7). This weakness, this difficulty, this problem, this failure dragged Paul down.

Right off we should say that we do not know what this thorn in the flesh was. Some say it was one thing and others another. Some say it was Paul's physical appearance. Some say it was an eye ailment, which they say was why an amanuensis—a sort of secretary—put pen to papyrus as Paul wrote his letters and Paul simply concluded them with his own hand. And when he did he used big letters (see Galatians 6:11; Philemon 19). Others say Paul's problem was malaria, which he had contracted in his travels. Some have even said his thorn in the flesh was his wife. I suppose it could be possible; sometimes some husbands and wives *are* like thorns in each other's lives. But this cannot be so from the Greek text. Paul called this thorn in the flesh "a messenger of Satan" (2 Cor. 12:7). The word "messenger" translates the Greek word *aggelos*, which elsewhere is translated *angel*. The word is masculine, and so it cannot refer to Paul's wife, if he had one, and we don't even know that for sure.

Simply put, we do not know what Paul's thorn in the flesh was. What we do know is that it was no laughing matter. It was one of those problems, troubles, failures, weaknesses that often is too painful to talk about. It hurt; it ached; and it troubled Paul greatly.

Paul knew that this "thorn" had a noble use, though. It kept him from the deadly sin of pride. As long as he had that thorn, Paul knew consciously and personally of his weakness.

Paul asked that the thorn be removed, but the answer was *no*. Paul asked three times, and the answer was still *no*.

Really, the answer was more than *no*. The answer was, "My grace is sufficient for you, for power is made perfect in weakness" (12:9). The thorn served to remind Paul of his weakness and of the uselessness of pride in himself. It also was an avenue through which the strong, sufficient, gracious power of Christ could operate. The thorn enabled Paul to know and keep knowing that he was only an earthen vessel but that Christ's transcendent power could fill him and motivate him (see 4:7).

So Paul said, "I will boast all the more gladly of my weaknesses, so that the power of Christ may dwell in me" (12:9). Furthermore, "I am content with weaknesses, insults, hardships, persecutions, and calamities for the sake of Christ; for whenever I am weak, then I am strong" (12:10).

Paul believed this statement on the basis of his experience in life. How can we make this truth our own? Let's look at the three foundation stones now.

Acknowledge the Tension
Between Pride and Weakness

All of us live in the tension between pride and weakness to one degree or another, and we would do well to acknowledge this tension. Paul lived in this tension.

We see this tension in our text, these first ten verses of 2 Corinthians 12. In the first six verses, Paul talked of the marvelous spiritual experience of a certain man in Christ. Likely this man was Paul himself. He was "caught up to the third heaven" (12:2), which was considered the highest heaven, according to one Jewish view. There in this mystical, ecstatic experience, Paul "heard things that are not to be told, that no mortal is permitted to repeat" (12:4).

Meanwhile, back on earth, Paul had this painful thorn in the flesh. So Paul lived in that tension between pride and weakness.

Further, Paul knew where the emphasis of his life must be placed. It must be placed on the weakness side, on the "thorn" side, rather than on the pride side. He said, " . . . I will not boast, except of my weaknesses" (12:5).

We live in this tension between pride and weakness, too, don't we? We know that if we do not have a good opinion of ourselves, no one else will either. We know that a striving for the best is what drives us on to be good students, good teachers, good athletes, good mechanics, good farmers, good doctors, good lawyers, and good whatever else. We are meant to be the best we can be, for Jesus' sake.

This is undeniably good. The danger is that we will think that we are the ones who are doing it out of ourselves and all by ourselves. We are at our best when we realize that the drive, power, and competence to be the best does not come *from* us but *through* us.

There is danger on the other side, too, from weakness. We can become so bogged down in our weakness, feeling so sorry for ourselves, that we drown in our own sorrows. We imprison ourselves in our hopelessness, lock the door from the inside, and swallow the key.

We were meant for more than this, though. We were meant to live the best kind of lives, lives that bring glory to God and help to our fellow human beings. And we can live such lives, even with our weakness and inadequacy.

So we live—and must live—in this tension between pride and weakness, between desiring the best and being unable to reach it fully because of some obstacle outside or inside. Acknowledging this tension is the first foundation stone for developing our greatest strength.

The second is this:

Develop the Trust Needed for Turning Weakness into Strength

What do you suppose Paul was thinking as he felt the pain of the thorn in his flesh? What do you suppose he thought as he asked the Lord not once, not twice, but three times to remove the hurt and it was not done?

Likely we do not have to imagine. We surely know from personal experience. Like us, Paul was thinking, agonizing, *Why did this have to happen to me? Why do I have to have this thorn? Why has life turned out this way? Why couldn't everything go smoothly, painlessly? Why couldn't I be the one for whom everything goes perfectly well, as it seems to for other people I know?*

But if Paul had such a thought, that thought was not where Paul remained. Because Paul trusted in God, Paul was able to avoid comparing himself to others. Rather, he was able to hear God saying, "My grace is sufficient for you, for power is made perfect in weakness" (12:9).

As with Paul, we have the word of our Lord that his grace is sufficient for us, too, for his power is made perfect in *our* weakness. Thus the second foundation stone for turning our weakness into strength is that we develop a vital trust in the Lord who loves us.

Here is the third foundation stone for developing your greatest strength:

Live Out the Truth
about Strength and Weakness

Hear again what Paul wrote in verse 10: "Therefore I am content with weaknesses, insults, hardships, persecutions, and calamities for the sake of Christ; for whenever I am weak, then I am strong." Paul not only said this, but he also lived out the truth about strength and weakness. That is, he lived, served, witnessed, ministered, and planned, not out of his strength, which was limited, but out of his weakness, which in a sense was unlimited. Living out of his weakness and need to rely on Christ opened the way for the power of Christ to operate within him and move through him to others. In another place, Paul said, " . . . We have this treasure in clay jars, so that it may be made clear that this extraordinary power belongs to God and does not come from us" (2 Corinthians 4:7).

What does this mean practically? I believe one important thing it means is to be willing to be personally vulnerable. It means admitting our imperfections and failures, not like endlessly replaying a broken record about an old surgical operation, but as people who are willing to acknowledge our hurts, nightmares, and failures as well as our hopes, dreams, and successes.

In our world that is driven so much by marketing, by never admitting errors, acknowledging failures is not easy to do. Even so, I can tell you that I have learned as much from my failures, especially those I've repeated two or three times, as from my successes. After all, it's only when we become willing to admit what we don't know and haven't done that we can get better, isn't it?

This calls for openness and honesty in the way we approach life. An outstanding psychologist told of talking to two patients at the mental hospital at which he served. One complained about how she had been railroaded into the hospital, how everyone was against her, and what a perfect life she had lived. After listening to all of this, the psychologist moved on to the next patient. He asked her how she happened to be in the hospital. She replied simply, "I goofed." Which do you think got well the quickest?[43]

We build lives by living out of our weaknesses so Christ can live in us and through us. We do not build lives by insisting that we are perfect.

You may be of a different political party from the person whom I am about to cite as an illustration of this truth. Even so, I encourage you just to hear his experience as a statement of a grieving human being. In September 2015, in the first week of the talk show, "The Late Show with Stephen Colbert," Colbert had as his guest Vice-President Joe Biden. Biden had lost his son to cancer only a few months before. Prodded by Colbert, Biden spoke of how his faith had helped him to deal with that great loss on top of other losses he had experienced in his life. Many were trying to get Biden to run for President. But Biden said, in an emotion-filled interview, that his grief was still too heavy to do that. He touched many lives as he acknowledged his weakness in the form of his great grief.[44]

Bryan Stevenson tells how he came to recognize something similar about himself. In doing so, he referred to this experience of Paul. In Stevenson's book, *Just Mercy*, he tells of his work as an attorney with the Equal Justice Initiative in trying to gain justice for people who had been wrongly convicted and for children who had been sentenced to lifetime imprisonment, among others. After he had lost a case, he was terribly discouraged. He wanted to quit. He gained strength to continue, though, when he came to this realization: "We are all broken by something. We have all hurt someone and have been hurt. We all share the condition of brokenness even if our brokenness is not equivalent."[45]

Stevenson continued: "We have a choice. We can embrace our humanness, which means embracing our broken natures and the compassion that remains our best hope for healing. Or we can deny our brokenness, forswear compassion, and, as a result, deny our own humanity."[46]

So it comes down to us and what we will do with both our strength and our weakness. Are we willing to admit that we, like Paul, live in the tension between pride and weakness? Are we developing the trust in God necessary for turning weakness into strength? Are we living out the truth about strength and weakness by learning to accept our weakness and even to live out of it?

If the answer to these questions is *yes*, then although we are weak, we are strong, for the grace of the Lord is sufficient for us. His power is made perfect in our weakness.

One of the beatitudes says, "Blessed are the poor in spirit, for theirs is the kingdom of heaven" (Matthew 5:3). That's another paradoxical statement, but it points to the truth of our text.

When we are weak, then we are strong. We can rely on God to make that happen.

21.
2 Samuel 7:1-14a
A Secure Future for God's People
Proper 11 (16): Eighth Sunday after
Pentecost

Sometimes we need reminding that all of our plans, even with the best of intentions, may not work out. In fact, life has a way of reminding us often, sometimes painfully, of that truth. Even so, sometimes we discover that there was always something better ahead than the plans we had so carefully made.

This truth is one of the truths in this rich passage that contains many avenues in it for understanding life, including our personal lives. The passage is about "a secure future for God's people." We desire that kind of future, too, don't we? The future the passage describes was more than even David, Israel's favorite king, envisioned, but he was part of its coming to pass.

Consider first where this passage fits in 1 and 2 Samuel. In 1 Samuel, the tribes of Israel had wanted to move beyond a loose-knit confederation of tribes to a monarchy as their neighbors had. The prophet and judge Samuel rather reluctantly had agreed to do that, with the Lord's reluctant agreement (1 Samuel 8). So, Samuel had anointed Saul as king.

Saul had promise at the beginning. After all, he was taller than everybody else (1 Sam. 9). But Saul had failed to fulfill his possibilities, and Samuel, led by the Lord, then had anointed a young fellow named David (1 Sam. 16). David was a shepherd boy who was good with a slingshot, and he also played a musical instrument. He also turned out to be an excellent military leader. Furthermore, he had charisma.

Samuel's anointing David had to face the small problem that Saul was still king. At the end of 1 Samuel, though, Saul was killed in battle.

The people then turned to David. David was anointed king over Judah (2 Samuel 2:1-4a). Then, after a time, to unite the nation, he was anointed king of all of Israel (2 Sam. 5:1-5). He made Jerusalem his capital (5:6-10) and brought the ark to Jerusalem (6:1-23).

Time passed, and David began to think about his life situation. Perhaps he began to think about his legacy. That's where the passage in 2 Samuel 7 begins.

Bible scholars have called this passage "the most important theological text in the books of Samuel and perhaps in the entire Deuteronomic History."[47] That history includes the books of Joshua, Judges, Samuel, and Kings. In addition, one of the greatest Old Testament scholars of today has called the words from the Lord in verses 4-16 "the most crucial theological statement in the Old Testament. . . ."[48]

So let us see what we can learn from this passage about God's working in David's life, in Israel's life, and in our lives. The lessons are many.

David's Plan (7:1-3)

Notice several things about this passage. What was David's situation? What did he now want to do? Why do you think he wanted to do that? Was this a good thing? How did the prophet Nathan reply?

David's situation was that, thanks to the Lord, he had defeated Israel's enemies, and he and the nation were enjoying a time of peace. Furthermore, he was living in a fine house, a house of cedar. Cedar was a wood of luxury. So David's house was luxurious.

Somehow it dawned on David to contrast where he resided—a substantial, luxurious house—to where "the ark of God" resided (7:2). David lived in a substantial, luxurious house, and the ark was in a tent.

The ark represented the presence of God. It was in essence a wooden box. Deuteronomy 10:1-5 indicates that the ark contained the tablets of the Ten Commandments (see also Exodus 25:10-22). A later tradition that is cited in Hebrews 9:4 indicates that it contained other objects as well.

The point is that the ark was sacred and revered, but it was kept in a tent. As David thought about the situation in his luxurious house, he came to realize that something was wrong with this picture.[49]

When David told the prophet Nathan his thoughts, David didn't have to spell it out in detail. He wanted to build a substantial structure for the ark. Nathan the prophet immediately replied, "Go and do all that you have in mind; for the LORD is with you" (2 Sam. 7:3).

The Lord's Response (7:4-17)

Nathan, though, should have talked to the Lord about David's idea before he so readily talked to David. That night, in some way, the Lord communicated quite clearly to Nathan that the Lord had other plans.

The Lord began by asking David in essence, *Why do you think I need a house?* And also, *Just supposing I want a house, why do you think you're the one to build it?*

The Lord pointed out that "since the day I brought up the people of Israel to this day, . . . I have been moving about in a tent and a tabernacle" (7:6). The implication may be that such a temporary structure fit well a God who moved and traveled. So God was content to be in a temporary structure. Or the implication may simply be that a house was unnecessary.

Moreover, when in time the Lord wanted a permanent structure, David was not going to be the one to build it. In this passage, God gave no reason for this restriction. In 1 Kings 5:3-4, though, Solomon said his father David could not build the temple for David was too busy fighting wars with Israel's enemies. In 1 Chronicles 22:6-9, this explanation from God about David appears: "You have shed much blood and have waged great wars: . . . you have shed so much blood in my sight on the earth." In essence, the meaning seems to be that David's reign was characterized by war, but Solomon was characterized by peace.

Thus, David's role and circumstances were different from Solomon's. Furthermore, the people themselves would be more settled and secure in Solomon's time, as verses 10-11 of 2 Samuel 7 suggest. The Lord would "appoint a place for my people Israel and will plant them, so that they may live in their own place, and be disturbed no more; and evildoers shall afflict them no more . . ." (2 Sam. 7:10). The emphasis seems to be on security, on not being threatened by enemies, for Israel already had been living in the land for some time.

So the Lord did like David's idea, but not at that time. There would come a time for building the house for the ark, the temple. God told David, "When your days are fulfilled and you lie down with your ancestors, I will raise up your offspring after you, who shall come forth from your body, and I will establish his kingdom. He shall build a house for my name . . . " (7:12-13). The reference here is to the building of the temple. Solomon, one of David's sons, would be charged with that task.

What God had in mind, though, was not just a physical house, a temple. Note the Lord's message to David in verse 11: " . . . the LORD declares to you that the LORD will make you a house." God was not speaking of a physical house. David already had a luxurious house. The word translated "house" can mean both a house—a physical structure in which to live—and a dynasty. So there's a play on words with the word "house." The Lord was speaking of making of David and his descendants a dynasty. In verse 12, the Lord explained this thought further by saying, "I will establish his kingdom."

Furthermore, that dynasty would continue. There would be punishment for the king who did wrong, but the dynasty would continue. In fact, verse 16 states that it would "be established forever."

We must look carefully at these promises, though, about Israel's having a place and about David's beginning a dynasty. Historically, Israel did lose its place. The Northern kingdom was conquered and the people taken into exile in the eighth century B.C., never to return. The Southern kingdom was conquered and the people taken into exile early in the sixth century B.C. However, they were allowed to return beginning later in that century, and so in general they were absent from the land only about fifty years. Furthermore, historically, there did cease to be a king in David's dynasty. The Davidic dynasty fell with the Exile in 587 B.C., with the brief exception of the return of Zerubbabel, a descendant of David, after the Exile (see Haggai 1:1).

What does this history say about these promises? Consider several ways to understand the promises.

First, look at the word "forever" in verses 13 and 16. We generally understand the word to mean something like *for all eternity*. The Hebrew word (*olam*), though, generally means a long, long time of indeterminate length (see Jeremiah 2:2). The time between David and the last king in his line, Zerubbabel, was more than 400 years—a long time but not forever.

Second, and more important, Scripture spells out elsewhere that this promise was conditional. It was not a blank check. For example, God made similar promises to Solomon in consecrating the temple in 1 Kings 9. In that chapter, though, God made clear the promise was not a blank check but rather had conditions. In 1 Kings 9:4-9, the Lord was quite clear that the promises were contingent on the word "if," as follows:

> As for you, if you will walk before me, as David your father walked, with integrity of heart and uprightness, doing according to all that I have commanded you, and keeping my statutes and my ordinances, then I will establish your royal throne over Israel forever, as I promised your father David, saying, 'There shall not fail you a successor on the throne of Israel."
>
> If you turn aside from following me, you or your children, and do not keep my commandments and my statutes that I

have set before you, but go and serve other gods and worship them, then I will cut Israel off from the land that I have given them; and the house that I have consecrated for my name I will cast out of my sight; and Israel will become a proverb and a taunt among all peoples. This house will become a heap of ruins; everyone passing by it will be astonished, and will hiss; and they will say, "Why has the LORD done such a thing to this land and to this house?" Then they will say, "Because they have forsaken the LORD their God, who brought their ancestors out of the land of Egypt, and embraced other gods, worshiping them and serving them; therefore the LORD has brought this disaster upon them."

For another example about the nature of God's promises, 1 Samuel 2 states that God had promised Eli that his family would be priests "forever." Because of the sins of Eli's sons, though, God annulled that promise. Samuel, not Eli's sons, would succeed Eli. God's promise was conditional on the faithfulness of Eli and his sons.

A third factor to consider in understanding this promise is even more important. Christians understand the promises in 2 Samuel 7 to refer to the Messiah. The Messiah continues David's dynasty and fulfills God's intent in the promises. The promises were not fulfilled by David's descendants continuing to occupy an earthly throne. Rather, the promises were fulfilled completely in Christ, the son of David (see Matthew 1:1; Acts 13:36).

So?

So how does this significant passage speak to us?

(1) It reminds us that our plans, even our best-intended plans, are not always God's plans.

(2) We must seek and keep seeking God's guidance in our plans.

(3) We must be prepared to bend our best-laid plans in accord with God's plans.

(4) We can and do influence the future, and we do it best when we are in tune with God's guidance.

(5) We should beware of an understanding of God's promises, even in Scripture, that puts God in a box and insists that God has to do this or that. We can easily be wrong. The prophet Jeremiah castigated the supposedly religious people who kept saying that since they had the temple, God was obligated to protect them (Jeremiah 7). Remember, too, that Jesus refused to jump from the pinnacle of the temple even though Scripture appeared to say that God would protect him if he did (Matthew 4:5-7).

(6) We must always respect and pay attention to the *if* in God's promises. God's promises generally are conditional on our obedience and faithfulness. As the gospel hymn states, we must "trust and obey, for there's no other way."[50]

211

(7) The thoughts in this and similar texts about a geographical place for Israel mean much to many Jewish people today, and rightly so, especially in light of the great suffering inflicted on them in the Holocaust as well as in persecutions in other places and times. Even so, we should be cautious about applying the promises in this text to modern political events. Engaging in such an effort can lead to questionable applications. For example, reliance on such promises can be used to justify actions of worldly politicians that may not be in accord with God's purposes. Even if these ancient promises are seen as having a measure of relevance to current events in the state of Israel, we must also avoid ignoring the *if* in these promises. Furthermore, we must be careful not to use these promises to justify actions harmful to other children of God, particularly the Palestinians. God loves them, too.

(8) Jesus is the ultimate fulfillment of the sentiments expressed in this promise. Jesus provides a secure place for God's people for now and forever and for here and elsewhere. This secure place is the place where God dwells with his people (Revelation 21:3). Moreover, God's people include people of "every nation, from all tribes and peoples and languages" (Rev. 7:9). There in that secure place, far beyond what happens in earthly kingdoms, God

> will wipe every tear from their eyes.
> Death will be no more;
> mourning and crying and pain will be
> no more,

for the first things have passed away
(Rev. 21:4).

22.

2 Samuel 11:26—12:13a
When the Truth Comes Out

Proper 13 (18): Tenth Sunday after Pentecost

Accountability is a key word these days. Paul spoke of the ultimate in accountability in Romans 14:12. There he wrote, " . . . Each of us will be accountable to God." That is, we are responsible to God for our actions and behavior. Just two verses earlier, in Romans 14:10, Paul had written pointedly, "For we will all stand before the judgment seat of God." That statement speaks of the highest of stakes in the matter of accountability.

David was the king, but even he had to face up to his personal responsibility and accountability for his actions. David is described as being a man after God's "own heart" (1 Samuel 13:14). This passage in 2 Samuel shows that he sometimes desired other things than that, too.

David's actions in these chapters were serious and sordid. They included lust, adultery, lying, murder, and an attempted cover-up. But the truth came out. It generally does, sometimes sooner rather than later and in the most inconvenient times. David was not perfect, far from it.

This passage is part of what is sometimes called either the court history of David or the succession narrative. It runs from 2 Samuel 11 to 1 Kings 2. David's public relations person or press secretary certainly didn't write it. It is not a puff piece filled with praise for David or excuses for his behavior. Rather it is brutally honest in its description of the happenings of David's reign and of David's actions. In these chapters, David is not God's fair-haired boy but a man who sins greatly. God forgives him, but David still has to suffer the temporal consequences of his actions. Much of the rest of 2 Samuel is about these tragic consequences in David's family, many if not all of them set in motion by David's sins in 2 Samuel 11. David's momentary delight turned into lifelong tragedy for himself and his family.

Furthermore, these chapters, especially chapters 11 and 12, demonstrate vividly and tragically the theme of all of the Deuteronomic history in the Books of Joshua, Judges, 1 and 2 Samuel, and 1 and 2 Kings. Why did Israel and then Judah later go into exile? Even David, who later would be looked up to as Israel's most revered king, sinned greatly.

Idle Time (11:1)

Verse 1 contains several lessons about human behavior. "In the spring of the year, the time when kings go out to battle, David" didn't go. Rather he sent his underlings. Did he think he was so powerful that he could delegate the task? Was he having a midlife crisis, having grown weary of the whole war thing? Was he just tired and wanted something new? Did he think he now had the luxury of delegating his military responsibilities to others? Had he forgotten that one of the reasons Israel wanted a king to begin with was to help them to defeat their enemies (see 1 Samuel 8:20).

Whatever the reason, David's action, or rather his non-action, reveals a bit of self-satisfaction. Plus it shows the danger of having too much time and too many resources at one's disposal plus an inflated view of oneself. David thought his identity was king, but that was only his role, in spite of his greatness. He was a human being responsible to God, but he might have thought he could get away with almost anything. He almost did.

Rabbah and the Ammonites, by the way, were on the east side of the Jordan. Joab was David's right-hand man. We might also call Joab David's hatchet man. Joab was willing to do the dirty work for David to keep David from soiling his reputation. He would figure further along in David's story, too.

Imagination in Action (11:2-5)

Here's the scene: a popular, virile man with time on his hands and with great power as the king; a beautiful woman who was not his wife. Of course, the woman was married, but David thought he could keep secret what he was about to do. After all, he was the king, and her husband was away in the army. Besides, her husband was a Hittite, not an Israelite. There's no indication Uriah's not being an Israelite was important to David,

217

though. He mainly banked on no one finding out what he had done.

The text says that David "was walking about on the roof of the king's house" (2 Samuel 11:2). The architecture of the day was such that roofs were flat. So people could walk around on them and even bathe on them.

Verse 4 is a key verse in what happened that day, of course. Furthermore, one word in that verse goes to the heart of what happened. "So David sent messengers to get her . . . ." The Hebrew word behind "to get" in 2 Samuel 11:4 is the word translated "take" in Samuel's warning in 1 Samuel 8:11-19 about what a king would do. Through Samuel God had warned the people that a king would *take*, and David *took*. Furthermore, the prophet Nathan used this word in his damning parable in 2 Samuel 12:4 and in his condemnation of David in 12:9, 10.

Some representations of this event do what many people do today in such situations—either blame the woman or at least make the woman complicit in what happened. When that is done, though, it reflects our own agendas and prejudices rather than what the Bible states and rather than the culture of the times. As a powerful king, David saw what he wanted—this beautiful woman. David then took what he wanted, just as Samuel had said would happen.

We must not go beyond the text to speculate about Bathsheba's motivations. The text is interested only in David's guilty behavior. David did what any king in that day could do: take. To speculate that Bathsheba was complicit when there is no evidence in the text to back up this claim is akin to blaming a rape victim for having been raped. Deuteronomy 22:22-24 does put some responsibility on the woman to cry out when she was being attacked, but who would help her in the king's palace?

Too, we must avoid turning David's incredibly brazen act of lust and power into romance as has sometimes been done. The text is about David and his desire for sex with a beautiful woman, with no hint of romance. Furthermore, in that day, a woman would have had little or no choice when the king wanted to *take*.

David seems to have forgotten or disregarded the seventh commandment. You know, the one about adultery. He would soon forget or disregard another one, too, the one just before that one, the one about murder. And he would engage in lying, another of the Ten Commandments, to cover up these sins.

Consider several more factors at this point in the story and how they figure into it. First, when David had seen Bathsheba bathing on her roof, "she was purifying herself after her period" (2 Sam. 11:4). Second, Bathsheba "conceived" (11:5). Third, she sent word to David, saying, "I am pregnant" (11:5). Put all of these factors together, and David, Bathsheba, and anyone else who could do simple math would know that the expected baby was not the child of Bathsheba and Uriah.

A Cover-Up Attempt (11:6-13)

Now the sixth commandment, the one about murder, enters the picture. David developed a plan to solve his problem.

David called his hatchet man, Joab, and told him, "Send me Uriah the Hittite" (11:6). At this point, Joab is pictured as simply obeying orders without a clue about why he was to return Uriah to Jerusalem.

So Uriah arrived back in Jerusalem to see David. Uriah, although a Hittite, would come across throughout these happenings as more trustworthy and more faithful than David.

David told Uriah, "Go down to your house, and wash your feet" (11:8). David even sent "a present" with Uriah. We don't know what it was. Perhaps a bottle of the finest wine? The words "wash your feet" in verse 8 are key here. They likely are a euphemism for sexual intercourse. David was encouraging Uriah, who likely had been away for weeks, to go home and enjoy sexual intercourse with his beautiful wife. David thought this plan might solve the problem of Bathsheba's pregnancy. Given the way the knowledge of pregnancy occurs, the timing would be a little off, but David evidently believed it would be close enough. He hoped so.

Uriah didn't go to his house, though, Rather he remained "at the entrance of the king's house with all the servants" (11:9).

When David found out what had happened, he question Uriah about why he did "not go down" to his house (11:11). Here Uriah's nobility shows through. Out of loyalty to Israel and his fellow soldiers, Uriah would not go to his home and enjoy pleasure with his wife. In addition, men on military battle duty were to abstain from sexual relations (1 Sam. 21:5; Deuteronomy 23:10).

David tried one more tactic. Perhaps he could get Uriah drunk enough that Uriah would forget his principles and go home to his wife. Alas for David, that didn't work either. Uriah slept with the servants again rather than going to see his wife.

The Last Resort (11:14-21)

David had one other idea for solving his problem. He "wrote a letter to" his hatchet man Joab. He instructed Joab to "set Uriah in the forefront of the hardest fighting, and then draw back from him, so that he may be struck down and die" (2 Sam. 11:15).

Joab was intensely loyal to David, but he likely suspected something was going on. After all, David was asking him to participate in the murder of Uriah and the cover-up.

So Joab did as instructed, and Uriah was killed in the battle. Joab covered up the plot in the instructions he gave to the messenger who was bringing the news to David. *If the king looks like he's angry about how I conducted the battle, just tell him Uriah is dead.* Joab knew that would solve any problem David might have with the way he had conducted the battle.

Joab in some sense already owned David. Now, though, Joab really owned him. David knew that Joab could testify against him if he wanted to do so. Later on, when David tried to replace Joab as the army commander, Joab simply ignored David and murdered his would-be replacement (19:13; 20:4-11).

Bad News and Good News (11:22-25)

The messenger delivered the message to David about the battle and Uriah's death. David nonchalantly replied that what happened was bad but not to worry about it. It was just collateral damage. These things happen.

Home Free at Last (11:26-27)

So, problem solved. David then brought the grieving pregnant widow to the palace. " . . . She became his wife, and bore him a son" (11:27). David was hoping people couldn't count the time between the marriage and the birth, or at least that the time was close enough that the birth wouldn't attract attention.

Here's the Truth (12:1-6)

But the problem was not solved. God didn't like it, and God sent Nathan to David with a story to consider.

Nathan was no court prophet. He allegiance was not to the government but to God. He wasn't beholden to big donors in his congregation to support the king no matter what. He was accountable only to God. His situation is a warning to us about the need for churches and religious leaders to maintain distance from political leaders and certainly not to enter into an arrangement with them that would negate or lessen their God-given role.

Nathan told David a story about a powerful man who took advantage of a poor man. Verse 4 capsules what happened. "Now there came a traveler to the rich man, and he was loath to take one of his own flock or herd to prepare for the wayfarer who had come to him, but he took the poor man's lamb, and prepared that for the guest who had come to him."

Nathan didn't have to ask David what he thought about the story. David knew his Bible. Because he did, he became angry at what had happened in the story. David even said, "As the LORD lives, the man who has done this deserves to die; he shall restore the lamb fourfold, because he did this thing, and because he had no pity" (12:6; see Exodus 22:1).

No Hiding from the Truth (12:7-13a)

Nathan's first words in verse 7 are among the most powerful in Scripture. They must have gotten David's immediate attention: "You are the man!"

Nathan then reminded David of how God had blessed him through the years. One thing Nathan was reminding David was that leadership is a role, not an identity. Furthermore, greatness as a leader only flows through a person and is not within that person. No matter how exalted one's title, there is a price to be paid for wrongdoing, eventually if not immediately. David was only a human being, and he was only a leader because God had made him one. God expected him to be faithful.

Nathan boldly said the unsayable in the presence of a powerful king who had just taken another man's wife, had her husband killed, and tried to cover up all he had done. Only a brave prophet who was independent of the king could have done what he did.

Nathan didn't stop with the accusation. He conveyed the judgment that was coming. There would be violence in David's own household. David's son Absalom would challenge his father's kingship and would even claim his father's wives, as kings did. The punishment for what David had done in secret would be broadcast to all.

David replied, "I have sinned against the LORD" (2 Sam. 12:13). At least David recognized his sin. Some people today don't. They even say they've never sought God's forgiveness because they never needed to. Here's a rule of life. If you insist you have never done anything wrong, you can't receive forgiveness, not even from God. But David confessed his sin (see Psalm 51, which depicts the spirit of David's confession).

David was spared the required punishment for adultery (see Deut. 22:23-24) and for murder (see Exodus 21:12). Even so, some punishment would and did come. The little child that had resulted from David's sin would die. I don't like that statement, for I don't like the idea that God takes away little babies because of the sins of the parent. Even so, that was what the prophet announced. We can be glad that this view was modified in the later prophets, Jeremiah and Ezekiel, especially in Ezekiel 18. People are responsible for their own sins, and the punishment is not passed down directly to the next generations.

So?

So what can we learn from this passage?

(1) Be where you're supposed to be, doing what you are supposed to do. If you are always doing what you are supposed to be doing, you won't be doing what you are not supposed to be doing.

(2) Remember that truth comes out, sooner if not later. What happened with David demonstrates the old saying, "O, what a tangled web we weave when first we practice to deceive!"[51] David's web became more and more tangled.

(3) Beware when you or anyone else has power. As a nineteenth-century British historian stated, "Power tends to corrupt; absolute power corrupts absolutely."[52]

(4) No one is above God's standard of right and wrong. Money, status, or power aren't enough to get around God. Wrongdoing always has consequences for everybody, no matter one's status.

(5) Beware of a close alliance between religion and government. From the time of Constantine in the fourth century on, such an alliance has been

more of a hindrance than a help to the Christian cause. It still is. The voice of religion is muted if not taken away entirely when religion lets itself depend on governmental support.

23.

Ephesians 4:1-16
Toward a Worthy Life

Proper 13 (18): Tenth Sunday after Pentecost

Sometimes parents have what we might call a nervous joy when they see their children who have become young adults moving out into life. They are joyful that they indeed are moving out into life, to be on their own. Where does the nervous part come in? Perhaps it comes in as they reflect on their own lives. They know how things can get sidetracked. They know, perhaps from painful personal experience, that things do not always turn out as smoothly as has been hoped and planned.

This sense of nervous joy is not limited to young people. At every stage and age of life, those of us who have experienced many of them know that things still do not necessarily work out as we had hoped and planned. The job becomes something other than it seemed it might be when we took it. The relationship that we thought was solid gets shaky. The perfect family about which we had dreamed somehow is not quite as perfect as we had dreamed. Even in retirement years, many learn that old age is not for sissies, as the cliché states.

These realities make the thoughts let loose by this Scripture passage even more important to consider. How can we lead a truly worthy life, "a life worthy of the calling to which [we] have been called" (Ephesians 4:1)? We can move toward leading a truly worthy life as we

Base Life on First Principles

David Brooks is a columnist for the *New York Times*. Sometimes his comments are political in nature, and sometimes they are more philosophical, even religious, in nature. You may like him, you may not like him, or you may have never heard of him. Whatever the case with you, any of those choices is okay, for I am mentioning him only in order to illustrate one point, and that's this. In one column, he distinguished between what he called "the résumé virtues and the eulogy virtues."[53] The "résumé virtues" are the kinds of things we put on our résumés or employment applications as we name the various markers of success we have experienced and accomplished in our lives. These kinds of things are the jobs we have held, the things we have done, and the education we have received. What, then, are the "eulogy virtues"? The "eulogy virtues" may make it into the obituary page, but they may not. The "eulogy virtues," though, are the kinds of things in the eulogy or in the conversations of the people who knew and loved you. These "eulogy virtues" likely are about what sort of person you were, how kind you were to this or that person, and how you made other people feel when they were around you.

I don't discount the "résumé virtues" as being unimportant. In fact, it may well be that both the "résumé virtues" and the "eulogy virtues" are important in their own ways. To receive a good education and to be entrusted with responsibilities in our work is not something to be downplayed or rejected. Brooks didn't say this, but we might think of the "résumé virtues" as perhaps in a sense providing the vehicle for living out the "eulogy virtues." When we are at our best, our résumé listings may be like the skeleton and the "eulogy virtues" may be like the flesh and blood.

It seems to me that Paul in this passage deals with the "eulogy virtues." When we have these right, the "résumé virtues" become more meaningful, and we are indeed moving toward a worthy life.

Paul mentioned "humility" first (Eph. 4:2). It's an important virtue, but it's not that easy to have. As the country song by Mac Davis goes, "Oh, Lord, it's hard to be humble, when you're perfect in every way."[54] As I say, humility is not that easy to have. It may be that when we think we're humble is when we most likely are not. Can you really be both humble and proud of being humble?

What is humility, anyway, though? Consider a few thoughts for getting at an answer to that question. Humility is knowing ourselves as we truly are, with our strengths and our weaknesses, and acting accordingly. It is acknowledging our creatureliness. Supremely, it is seeing for certain that we do not measure up to Jesus.

Paul next mentioned "gentleness" (4:2). Gentleness refers to a balanced, God-controlled life. "Gentleness" means being in control of both your physical and your inward appetites. It means not climbing over folks or kicking them aside to get what you wish.

The third item on this list of "eulogy virtues" is "patience" (4:2). We can understand "patience" as having two senses.

"Patience" refers to endurance, meaning not giving up. All of us likely need to learn patience in this sense. Living the most joyful life, or at least just surviving, depends on this. Sometimes we give up too easily when what we really need to do is recognize that good things sometimes require a lot of hard, grinding effort over time. Only on television do hard problems get solved in twenty-two minutes, an hour, or even two.

Paul next called for "bearing with one another in love." Sometimes it's hard to do both of those things—love others and also bear with them—isn't it? But that's really what a great deal of relating to our fellow human beings requires. Relationships require extending positive good will even to people whom we may not like all that much—at the moment, anyway. A quote attributed to Augustine says, "What does love look like? It has the hands to help others. It has the feet to hasten to the poor and needy. It has eyes to see misery and want. It has the ears to hear the sighs and sorrows of [people]. That is what love looks like."

The other "eulogy virtue" Paul mentioned is the "peace" that issues in "unity." Read the letters of the New Testament and you will see that the early Christians had a lot of characteristics with which we are familiar. They had their dislikes and their irritations, largely brought about by other people. They had intense disagreements, including disagreeing about who should be included in their fellowship and how.

Continue reading the New Testament and several truths become clear about the Christian life. First, Christ makes people new creations. Second, people have to work at letting this newness fill their lives. Third, they—and we—can do that and thus learn to "maintain the unity of the Spirit in the bond of peace." We can learn to get along with one another and even be united.

It's sometimes disappointing to me that I haven't gotten nearly as far along in the Christian life as I had hoped I would by this time. Sometimes I still say things to people that I wished I hadn't said, and sometimes I don't say things that I wished I *had* said. Sometimes I still do things I wished I hadn't done, and sometimes I don't do things I wished I had done.

Even so, these "eulogy virtues" of Paul give me some things to live toward. Are these things— humility, gentleness, patience, love, unity—on your list, too?[55]

231

Reach Out

In this passage, Paul gave us another way we can lead a truly worthy life. He did that in his discussion on gifts. The bottom line is that we were never meant to be wrapped up in ourselves. As someone has said, people who are all wrapped up in themselves make very small packages. We were meant to reach out to others.

Paul discussed spiritual gifts in more detail in another place in his writings. There, Paul was clear that gifts are meant to be used, not for ourselves, but for "the common good" (1 Corinthians 12:7).

This quality is an important one in growing as people, especially as adults. The mark of maturity, or at least in maturing, since probably few if any of us ever arrive at complete maturity, is the point at which we cease to be as preoccupied with what other people, even parents, can do for us and decide to become people who care for, bless, and guide other people ourselves. Maturity can be measured by what dominates our lives.

Your life—a worthy life—is meant to be a life that reaches out. It sounds a bit like a cliché, but each of us has been given at least one gift. It needs to be said often, though, to get us at last to hear, and to remind us, for many people so easily lapse into feelings of worthlessness.

A professor of mine, Dr. Kenneth Chafin, tells of receiving a book that had a blank page. Page 67 in the book was blank because of a printing error.

Dr. Chafin was telling someone else about it, and he was surprised at what the person told him. The person said, "I identify with that blank page." Dr. Chafin said he began checking around and found that a lot of people felt like that—that they were page 67, blank.[56]

Paul said otherwise, though, in this passage. We have all been given gifts, and we all are expected to reach out to others with them.[57]

Grow Up in Every Way into Christ

Leading a truly worthy life also calls for growing up in every way into Christ. We hear much talk these days about people who are spiritual but not religious. That generally means that they are spiritual but have no regard for religion as exemplified by churches.

Such a view—simply being spiritual—is incomplete and even insufficient, but it does point churches and church leaders to something very important that we have lost or at least obscured. That is this. The center of our church life must not be church life but Jesus. We become just another institution when we take our eyes off Jesus as our pattern, our ideal, "the pioneer and perfecter of our faith" (Hebrews 12:2).

The expression "What would Jesus do?" can treated in a trite way. If we asked it more sincerely, though, we might well solve many problems in our lives and in our churches. We should also ask, "What would Jesus have *me* do?" We are to follow not merely principles but the Person who embodies and taught these principles.

If we aimed more surely at growing up in every way into Christ, there would be at least two results. First, we would indeed "no longer be children, tossed to and fro and blown about by every wind of doctrine" (Eph. 4:14). We would not be dependent on others' ideas and thoughts but on Christ's. Second, each of us would take our own unique place in the body of Christ. We would not be all alike, but we would fit in our unique place, like the parts of a healthy body. We would form a team joined in a common purpose on the basis of a common love for Jesus.

The vision for life we see in this Scripture passage can be our life, a worthy life, as we base our lives on what is truly important, as we reach out with our gifts to other people, and as we truly grow up in every way into Christ.

24.
2 Samuel 18:5-9, 15, 31-33
Nightmare in the Daytime
Proper 14 (19): Eleventh Sunday after
Pentecost

Years ago one of my favorite storytellers, Garrison Keillor, told a story on his radio program *A Prairie Home Companion* about a man and a woman from a small town. Each of them worked for a different company. They were married but not to each other.

Each of them, unbeknown to the other, was assigned by their company to go on a business trip to a large city. As they boarded the train, they unexpectedly saw each other. They knew each other, and they decided to sit together on the journey. They discovered their destination was the same. In fact, they would be staying in the same hotel.

What happened on the rest of the trip seems to fit with the story of David in 2 Samuel. They took a taxi together to the hotel. As they arrived at the hotel, they decided to have dinner together that evening in the hotel restaurant. The man and the woman were both attractive and were about the same age. They both had children.

The story tells of what was going through the minds of the couple as they had dinner together. What was going through their minds was what they might do together there that night in the big city in the same hotel and how the business trip might turn into something more. After all, they were far from home and anonymous in the big city. Who would know?

Each, though, began to think about their spouse, their children, their neighbors, and their friends. Each of them came to the same realization. Neither of them wanted to act in a way that potentially and even likely would bring sorrow and tragedy into their lives and the lives of so many others.

Unfortunately, David did not reach the point of thinking such thoughts about how his lust for Bathsheba might bring tragedy. He simply acted on his impulses and used his power as king to take her for himself. He even had her husband murdered. All of this is described in 2 Samuel 11. The rest of 2 Samuel is about the tragedy that David's actions brought on himself, his family, and his country. Shakespeare didn't write his plays until about 2,500 years later, but the rest of David's life became a Shakespearean tragedy.

From 2 Samuel 11 to 1 Kings 2 is sometimes called either the court history of David or the succession narrative. It runs from 2 Samuel 11 to 1 Kings 2. David's public relations person or press secretary certainly didn't write it. It is not a puff piece filled with praise for David or excuses for his behavior. Rather it is brutally honest in its description of the happenings of David's reign and of David's actions. In these chapters, David was not God's fair-haired boy but a man who sinned greatly.

Under pressure from the prophet Nathan, David confessed his great sins, and God forgave him. Even so, David still had to suffer the temporal consequences of his actions. Beginning with 2 Samuel 13, the remainder of the book is about these tragic consequences in David's family, all set in motion by David's sins in 2 Samuel 11. David's momentary delight turned into lifelong tragedy for himself and his family.

As a succession narrative for the monarchy, these chapters show how two rivals for the throne were eliminated—Amnon and Absalom. Later, the early chapters of 1 Kings will tell of the two remaining rivals—Adonijah and Solomon.

Furthermore, these chapters demonstrate vividly and tragically the theme of all of the Deuteronomic history in the Books of Joshua, Judges, 1 and 2 Samuel, and 1 and 2 Kings. A major them of these books is focused on answering this question: *Why did Israel and then Judah go into exile?* The answer in 2 Samuel 11 through 1 Kings 2 is that even David, who later would be looked up to as Israel's most revered king, sinned greatly.[58]

The Tragedy Continues (13:20-21)

The tragedy in the life of David did not end when Naaman the prophet forcefully called him to account and to confess his wrongdoing. David saw the tragedy of his actions working out first in the little baby that came from his affair (see my comments on this incident in 22. 2 Samuel 11:26—12:13a, "When the Truth Comes Out"). It continued in the lives of David's adult children.

Chapter 13 tells the sordid story of David's adult son Amnon. Amnon could not control his lust for his half-sister, Tamar. He lied about a supposed illness so he could be with her. When she refused him, he raped her and destroyed her life. Does any of this sound familiar from David's history?

Tamar's brother, Absalom, found out what had happened. At first, in 2 Samuel 13:20, he seems not to acknowledge the depths of his sister's suffering. In 2 Samuel 13:22, we see, though, that "Absalom hated Amnon, because he had raped his sister Tamar."

In verse 21, we see also that David himself "became very angry, but he would not punish his son Amnon, because he loved him, for he was his firstborn." As the firstborn, Amnon was first in line to succeed David as king. David was angry, but he did nothing. Absalom was angry, and after a time he would take action.

Can you see a collision coming involving David, Absalom, and Amnon? What do you think each of them was feeling? Amnon's evil act, Absalom's hatred for him, and David's inaction were about to collide.

Absalom's Revenge (13:30-33)

Absalom bided his time for two years. Then he set up a situation to trap Amnon and take revenge against him. Absalom planned a party at his estate. He invited his father, all of his father's sons, and his father's attendants. David excused himself, saying that such a gathering would be a great deal of trouble, too much trouble, in fact. David continued his hands-off pattern and indicated that he and his attendants would not be coming.

Absalom continued to pursue the matter, though, and eventually persuaded David to let Amnon and David's other sons go to the party. The party turned into an assassination of Amnon as revenge for Amnon's rape of Tamar and David's favoritism for Amnon and refusal to punish him.

At first, the report came to David that Absalom had killed all of David's sons. As if to soften the blow, the second and accurate report came that "Amnon alone is dead" (2 Sam. 13:33). Not much comfort there.

Absalom Challenges David (14:25—15:10)

Absalom left the country after Amnon's assassination. David mourned the loss of Amnon, and then "the heart of the king went out, yearning for Absalom (13:39).

At last, through some wheeling and dealing by Joab, David's military commander, David was persuaded to allow Absalom to return. But David would not see him. "So Absalom went to his own house, and did not come into the king's presence" (14:24).

Absalom would not be denied, though. He was exceedingly handsome and had a great head of hair.

Absalom got Joab's attention and insisted that Joab persuade David to receive him back. Joab did just that.

So Absalom came back home, and David at last received him. That was not enough for Absalom, though. He became known in the nation as the go-to guy to get something done. Thus, "Absalom stole the hearts of the people of Israel" (15:6).

Absalom had laid the foundation for what he would do next. He would become king, replacing his father, David. He wouldn't even wait for his father to die.

So Absalom asked David to allow him to go to Hebron to worship. What was really to happen there, though, was that the leaders of the various tribes would proclaim Absalom king. Hebron was the city where the leaders of Judah had gathered to proclaim David king years earlier.

When David realized that Absalom was orchestrating a coup, he and his entourage fled. Chapters 16 and 17 tell some of the details of the conspiracy and David's actions to thwart it eventually.

The Final Battle, the Final Tragedy
(18:5-15, 30-33)

David's military leaders persuaded him not to engage in the battle against Absalom's forces himself. His last instructions to them were, "Deal gently for my sake with the young man Absalom" (18:5). Everybody heard what he said.

In the battle, David's forces defeated Absalom's forces. Absalom himself met a gruesome fate. His "head" got caught in a tree, and he was left hanging there (18:9). We cannot help thinking that his full head of hair didn't help.

When Joab heard what had happened to Absalom, his first response was not, *Well, be careful in freeing him. The king told us not to hurt him.* Kindness was not Joab's strong suit. So he did not hesitate to kill Absalom for instigating the coup. For Joab, this was no time for petty concerns about morality or even for carrying out the king's order not to harm his son.

The news of Absalom's death was conveyed to David. David asked the messenger with the news, "Is it well with the young man Absalom?" (18:29). The messenger responded in indirect language, "May the enemies of my Lord the king, and all who rise up to do you harm, be like that young man" (18:32). With that roundabout statement, David knew the answer, and he was shattered.

Any parent who has ever experienced tragedy because of a child understands David's feelings. "The king was deeply moved, and went up to the

241

chamber over the gate, and wept; and as he went, he said, 'O my son Absalom, my son, my son Absalom! Would I had died instead of you, O Absalom, my son, my son!'" (18:33).

So?

The renowned writer of short stories in an earlier day, O. Henry, has a short story called "The Guilty Party." As it begins there's a little girl who wants her father to care for her and to pay her some attention. But he won't. He ignores her and treats her shabbily.

The little girl grows up, gets in with the wrong crowd, murders her fiancé for two-timing her, commits suicide, and winds up in a court scene in the afterlife. The arresting angel suggests to the court officer angel that they send her on to eternal punishment. After all, he says, "The wages of sin is death. Praise the Lord."

The court officer angel fusses at the arresting angel and says to him that he has the wrong person. He's made a false arrest. The court officer angel then says to the arresting angel,

> The guilty party you've got to look for in this case is a red-haired, unshaven, untidy man, sitting by the window reading, in his stocking feet, while his children play in the streets.[59]

So, what regrets do you think David, the father of both Amnon and Absalom, might have had as he experienced the tragedies of these chapters? What do you think David might have wished he had done better?

Moreover, what are some things these chapters say about parenting? It's important to remember, of course, as we consider our own parenting, that there comes a time when children do make their own decisions. Thus, grown-up children cannot and must not trace all their decisions and actions to their parenting. Parents affect the lives of their children tremendously, but we cannot blame all of our shortcomings on our parents.

So what if our parenting days are over, way over? What does this sad time in David's life say at that stage of life? To begin with, we need to remember that there are no perfect parents. Even good parents generally do the best they can and know how to do at the time. Beyond that, if we know that we failed greatly, it is not too late for God's forgiveness and for us to take action to make things closer to right as best we can. God can bring about good, even out of chaos. That's what God did at the very beginning of it all, in fact. That's what God can still do.

If your parenting days are past, way past, here's something else to think about and maybe do. Growing up, I don't recall doubting my parents' love for me. So I felt security and love from my parents as I grew up. However, I also don't recall hearing the words, *I love you*, very often if ever, although I want to think that I did hear them from my mother.

When my parents grew old, though, and I was middle-aged, something changed. The change was major, as I see it. On my trips home several times a year, they began to make a point of saying, *We love you*. They even pointedly told me on at least one occasion that they wanted to be sure I knew that they loved me. This change and these words brought joy to me.

If all your children are grown and your parenting days are past, you can still do something memorable that will last for eternity. Tell your children, your grandchildren, your great-grandchildren, your dearest relatives, especially if you have no children, that you love them. A side benefit of doing this is that, as Scripture says, when such love is genuine, " . . . Love covers a multitude of sins" (1 Peter 4:8).

25.

1 Kings 19:4-8
Finding the Way Out and Up

Proper 14 (19): Eleventh Sunday after
Pentecost

When most people hear this passage of Scripture about Elijah's very bad day—and more—it's not hard for them to identify with at least some if not all of it. Elijah was down, way down, and running on empty. Most of us, if not all of us, know what that means and what it feels like. Most of us know what it's like to feel at least somewhat depressed and down. This experience is not by any means limited to a few, although some seem not to go as far down as others or have learned to disguise it better. Is there anything we can do about it? If so, what is it?

Let me say that I don't want to appear in the least to make light of this. Some levels of depression can be so serious that professional help is needed, including medical treatment, to get relief. Consider what I'm going to say as the first solutions to try. I believe them to be sound and to be based both on Scripture and on current best practices. So do try to put into practice the suggestions I'm going to make, but, please, if the sadness of depression persists, talk with a professional, perhaps your doctor, about what you are experiencing, and don't give up. Help is available.[60] Now back to Elijah.

Elijah's Up and Down Experiences

As we look at this experience of the prophet Elijah, we discover that the Bible knows well what we are talking about. Are you surprised to learn that Elijah, one of God's greatest, bravest prophets, had an experience in which he felt down, terribly down, exhausted, the deepest shade of blue you can imagine, running on empty? In a way, we cannot help but be surprised, because so much of Elijah's life was *up*, not *down*.

Refresh your memory about Elijah and you will see this pretty clearly. The Elijah we see portrayed so vividly in 1 and 2 Kings was a powerful figure.

When we first meet Elijah in 1 Kings 17, he was delivering a fearsome message to the most powerful person in Israel, King Ahab. Elijah said, "As the LORD the God of Israel lives, before whom I stand, there shall be neither dew nor rain these years, except by my word" (1 Kings 17:1). That blunt statement was definitely not what the king wanted to hear, but that's the way it was. Likely the people cried over and over to Baal—considered the god of fertility in crops, animals, and people—but the rain didn't come. Elijah had said it wouldn't and furthermore had said that the rain wouldn't come until he said it would. Take that, king.

Next we see Elijah working a miracle for a poor widow whose flour and oil, her means of subsistence, had run out. After Elijah came around, though, no matter how much she used, there was always enough for her needs (see 17:8-16).

Then we see Elijah working an even more spectacular miracle. He raised a widow's dead son to life (see 17:17-24).

After that, we see Elijah confronting 400 prophets of Baal in a contest on Mount Carmel. Elijah taunted them with their powerless god, Baal, who did not send fire to burn the sacrifice. Then, in a spectacular manner, Elijah proved that his God was really *the* God. Elijah drenched the altar with water, not once, not twice, but three times. Only then did Elijah ask God to send the fire. And God did (see 18:1-35).

Finally Elijah informed King Ahab that it was going to rain at last, after three years of drought. Elijah further told King Ahab that if Ahab didn't get going his chariot was going to get stuck in the mud (see 18:41-46).

Elijah was a person of power. All of these were *up* experiences.

Then something happened. A woman named Jezebel was the king's wife, but she was no lady. She threatened to take Elijah's life (see 19:1-2).

This threat frightened Elijah as nothing else had. He fled for his life. He fled from the north end of Palestine to the south and then went into the wilderness a day's journey. Then he sat down under a broom tree. In truth he was way under the broom tree, as low as he could get. He was empty.

Then Elijah prayed a silly prayer. He asked that he might die. If that were what Elijah wanted, why didn't he just stay and let Jezebel take care of that prayer request? Elijah was exhibiting a severe case of being down, depressed, exhausted, empty. He wasn't making good sense.

A little later, after our Scripture text, we find Elijah in a cave. Twice he said to God, "I alone am left, and they are seeking my life, to take it away" (19:10, 14).

What do you see in this account for you? To begin with, the experience of running on empty, of being down, happens to almost everybody at some time or other, including a prophet of God. Further, you can do something about it. There is a way out and up from being down. That way is what we want to look at and find out about.

Finding a Way Out and Up

Some truths in this experience of Elijah can help us find the way out and up. Let's not take this first one too far, but it's interesting to note that Elijah only got ready to get up from being down when he stopped running.

Sometimes we are indeed running too far and too fast in our lives, and we need to slow down and retreat for a time. Someone described the lifestyle of too many people in our culture these days in three words: *hurry, worry, bury.* To find the way out and up from being down, we may need to stop running, to let go of some things, to say *no* to some things that no longer really need doing or to which we perhaps should never had said *yes*, to take some time off, to refresh and refocus our lives. Like most things, we shouldn't go overboard on this and completely isolate ourselves; that wouldn't be healthy either. It wasn't for Elijah.

A second truth from Elijah's experience is that we will need to exert some effort if we are to find the way out and up from being down. Through an angel, the Lord instructed Elijah to do one thing, "Get up and eat" (19:5). Elijah needed to do that. He had run and run and run seventeen miles from Mount Carmel to Jezreel. Then he had journeyed from the north end of Israel to Beer-sheba in the south. At last, out of exhaustion and depression, he slept. God woke him up and said, "Get up." That command to do one thing was the step Elijah needed to take to get up from being down.

Often in our experience of being down, running on empty, we think we ought to do something but feel we will have to take on the whole world at once. It would be better to start with the one thing that lies directly before us. In Elijah's case, that was just to get up and eat. That was all, but he had to exert the effort to do that one thing.

A third truth in Elijah's experience is that we see that taking care of our physical needs is important. Elijah slept, refreshing his body, and Elijah ate, nourishing his body. Let us not forget the importance of both of these actions. They represent the overall acts of care we are to give to our physical bodies. After all, the meaning of the incarnation, of God's being somehow embodied in Jesus of Nazareth, is that our bodies, our physical bodies, are important.

Many years ago I heard the great preacher, Dr. Howard Thurman, preach. I still recall much of what he said that day. One memorable illustration he gave was of going to his doctor for his checkup. The doctor told Dr. Thurman he was doing pretty well, but that he did need to lose about ten pounds. Thurman said he looked at his doctor and recognized that his doctor needed to lose a lot more than ten pounds, more like *fifty* pounds. Thurman said to himself, *My doctor thinks his body knows he is a doctor.* That is, the doctor thought he was immune from giving attention to his own health just because he was a doctor.

Do you think your body knows you are a wonderful person, doing many wonderful things and perhaps being indispensable to many people? Maybe, but likely your body would appreciate your taking the best care of it possible. It's the only physical body you will have. The rest we get or don't get, the amount and kind of nourishment we give to our bodies, the physical activity we get—all are important to our bodies and to our lives in general.

Another truth we can see in Elijah's experience is the need to tell somebody what we are feeling. People whose dear ones have taken their own lives often find themselves saying, *If he or she had only told us. . . .* The truth is that talking to a trusted friend or professional about our deep and dark feelings can often help us get past them. Yes, tell God; that's what Elijah did, although God would already have known. But also tell a trusted friend, professional counselor, or your physician about it. Sometimes we need God in a human being we can see and who will listen and provide help.[61]

The rest of Elijah's experience reveals that Elijah did at least one other thing to find the way out and up. He expanded his vision. When Elijah was down, his vision was limited to himself and his fear of Jezebel. One reason we sometimes feel down is that we have lost our perspective on things.

Elijah needed to expand his vision to take account of the greatness of God. God told Elijah in his depression, "Go out and stand on the mountain before the LORD for the LORD is about to pass by" (19:11).

Elijah did that. As he stood there, a strong wind came and broke the rocks in pieces. An earthquake came and after the earthquake, a fire. But the Lord was not in any of these. The mighty Lord of the wind, the earthquake, and the fire came in "the sound of sheer silence" (19:12) or "a still small voice" (KJV). The Lord came in the silence.

Do you recall Holman Hunt's painting of Jesus knocking at the door, seeking entrance? It's called "The Light of the World," and the larger version is in St. Paul's Cathedral in London. I was delighted to see it in person a few years ago.[62] There's a story of a child viewing the painting with her parents. She asked, *Why don't the people open the door to Jesus?* And then she answered herself, *Maybe they're not at home, or maybe they're not paying attention because they're doing other things, or maybe the television is on so loud that they cannot hear the knock.* If we are to hear the Lord who comes in "a still small voice' or "a sound of sheer silence," we will have to learn to listen better, won't we?

A part of this matter of expanding our vision and getting a better perspective on things is to expand our view of people, to see that we are not alone but that other people are with us. When Elijah was down under the broom tree, he thought he was all by himself in worshiping the true God, that everybody had started worshiping Baal but him. God corrected him by pointing out that he still had 7,000 people in Israel who didn't worship Baal. That number—7,000—means that there were lots more people than Elijah who worshiped the true God. Elijah just hadn't been able to let himself see them. Elijah was not alone, and he could get help and strength from his fellow human beings.

When we feel we are the only ones and we must go it alone, life can seem terribly hard. But when we know there are others with whom we can share our burdens, we are on the way out and up.

If you're down, you can make a good start today toward finding the way out and up. We don't have to be down, running on empty. The good news of the gospel is that there is an *up*, and this *up* is accessible to us through God's grace and God's power.

26.
Mark 7:1-8, 14-15, 21-23
Clean Hands or Pure Hearts

Proper 17 (22):
Fourteenth Sunday after Pentecost

When I was a child, my father would let it be known that supper was ready and it was time to eat by saying to my brother and me, *All right, boys, time to wash your hands.* We knew to do that, and that's what we did.

Lest little boys and grown men, mainly, mistake the meaning of this passage of Scripture about the washing of hands, let me be clear that it is not a proof text for refusing to wash your hands before dinner or for not washing the dishes afterward. The controversy at your house may be about washing hands and dishes, but the controversy in this passage of Scripture was not about physical cleanliness but about religious rituals, traditions, and customs.

Rather, it was about questions like these: Was following religious rituals and traditions a necessary part of an authentic relationship with God, or did an authentic relationship with God come in another way? Was God satisfied with clean hands and dishes, or did God desire something else?

Tradition, Tradition

The Gospel of Mark portrays the Pharisees as living under some rather restrictive and rigid religious rules. They believed that these rules had been passed down to them by word-of-mouth all the way from Moses himself. The intention of these rules, called the oral tradition, was to build a fence around the written law so that no one would ever transgress it. They felt that by keeping these rigid rules about the most minute details they could be certain they were living a holy life and their deeds made them fully acceptable to God. If they kept the rituals and the rules, then they had no worries.

The oral tradition had been passed down from great teacher to great teacher, from generation to generation. The theme of the tradition was, *This is the way you do it, this business of religion, if you truly want to be acceptable to God, if you do not want our nation to be destroyed and sent into exile again, and if you want the Messiah to come.* With good intentions, the religious leaders had analyzed and sliced life into manageable little pieces. By handling even these little details properly, they believed they could be certain they were living life properly and were properly acceptable to God.

The particular tradition that began this controversy with Jesus in this text was that of the ritual washing of hands. The Pharisees noticed that Jesus' disciples did not follow the hand-washing ritual prescribed in the oral tradition and that the disciples thus ate with unclean hands, religiously speaking.

This situation reminds me of a cartoon I saw once. The cartoon pictured a man exiting a public restroom. A neon sign above the door began flashing, *Did not wash hands.* Now, we don't know everything about the disciples' hygiene practices or about their table manners. They were fishermen and tax collectors and such. But their hygiene practices and their table manners were not the problem.

The religious leaders were not concerned with physical cleanliness but with ceremonial cleanliness. Before every meal, the hands had to be washed in a certain way. That way was prescribed to the smallest detail, even down to the minimum amount of water to be used. The Pharisees wanted to cleanse themselves from any contact with unholy things, unholy actions, and especially unholy people like Gentiles and other people they considered sinners. The Pharisees believed that any truly religious person would follow this tradition carefully, meticulously, and religiously, without fail.

Perhaps you think this practice occurred long ago—and it did. Perhaps you think this concern for tradition is out of touch with you and your life—but it isn't. We should not minimize the hold that tradition, custom, and, yes, ritual may have on us, too.

Most of us move within the traditions and customs of family, community, peer group, and religious group more than we would like to admit. We may think we are living in freedom and doing what we wish to do, but we live a great deal out of our backgrounds, traditions, rituals, rules, and customs that have come to us from and through others. Even when we rebel against these traditions and customs, often we are not really thinking for ourselves and forging our own paths. We are simply exchanging one set of traditions for another.

Tradition has a powerful hold on us. The psychologists are telling us that you and I carry around within us what we might call pre-recorded tapes in our heads. Our childhood experiences are there. The traditions we absorbed from our parents and other sources are there. The result is that often, if we are not careful and purposefully thoughtful, we do not think for ourselves as individuals. We just play the pre-recorded tape and live a life of re-runs, we might say. To an extent, our past influences and experiences continue to live in us and through us.

If your family and other background experiences are telling you today that Christian living is one thing, you will be hard pressed to change that idea. If a family or community or church has had a certain tradition about morality or about Christian living, it will affect you. You may rebel against it, but it will still affect you. You can change its effect, but doing so will require some effort, maybe a lot of effort.

Of course, we should not forget that tradition may have great value for us. There are good traditions, after all.

Even Jesus had customs, habits, and patterns of life. Surely he did not act on them without having examined them, but the Scripture does tell us that Jesus "went to the synagogue on the sabbath day, as was his custom" (Luke 4:16). Elsewhere we read that as the crowds gathered to Jesus, "as was his custom, he again taught them" (Mark 10:1).

Let us remind ourselves again, too, that the intentions of the Pharisees in this matter of tradition were not bad, however perverted they might have become in practice. The Pharisees were seriously concerned about right relationship with God.

Whatever tradition you yourself have may have its good points. For one thing, tradition enables us to make up our minds about a matter rather than having to consider it again and again, every time it comes up. If there are services of the church that you attend or do not attend, then you do not have to decide what you will or will not do when the time comes. If you perform certain actions by habit, then you do not have to think about them. You just do them. When A occurs, you just do B, the next thing in the tradition, with no thought required. If you hold a certain opinion about a certain set of people, then no gray matter needs to be expended over how to relate to them in a given instance.

If the traditions you follow are good traditions, you may save yourself some trouble, too. You may keep yourself from being led into trouble, simply by virtue of the fact that your background tells you a certain kind of behavior is not right. Your people just don't do those things.

Problems with Traditions

But there can be real problems with our traditions, rituals, and customs. According to this text, Jesus wants us to face these problems. What are they?

One problem with tradition is that it gets outdated and old-fashioned, meaning that it does not speak to current life. We used to sing about the *old-time religion*. Since it was good enough for Paul and Silas, it's good enough for me, so the song went.

Let's look at that matter about Paul and Silas, though, as an example. Paul and Silas and Barnabas and the rest of that first-century crowd were anything but old-fashioned. They were the creative people of their day, challenging Jews and Gentiles and all the world to change. That bunch, our spiritual ancestors, in fact kept turning the world upside-down, or right-side up. They were anything but static, set-in-their-ways, status-quo type folks. Why? Because they knew and followed Jesus and not merely some outdated tradition.

A lay leader whom I knew, a clear-thinking, committed Christian, once told me that when some spiritual practice he was doing started to be a habit, he changed it. He said that if the practice used to be helpful and good but he found himself wondering why he was doing it, he started trying to change it, either by breathing new life into it or changing it to something better.

A ninety-seven-year-old woman was talking to a friend of mine who was her pastor. This ninety-seven-year-old woman told her pastor that her church had to be willing to make some changes if it wanted to minister to the present and in the future. Hooray for her. She knew that a problem with tradition is that it gets outdated and out of touch.

Another problem is that tradition all too readily begins to identify itself with perfection and becomes superficial, even hypocritical, in the process. This had happened with the religion of this passage of Scripture.

Jesus pointed out to the Pharisees that they were so concerned with keeping the tradition that they had rejected the commandment of God. Moses had commanded, "Honor your father and your mother" (7:10). The Pharisees, though, approved of a custom known as *Corban*. That is, a man could say *Corban* about his property, and it would be considered to be dedicated to God. However, the man could still use it as his own. But if his family needed help, the person could greedily and piously point out that his money and property were all tied up, for he had given them to God.

The Pharisees believed it was more important for the man to keep the vow, hypocritical though it was, than to help people. According to the

Gospel of Mark, the customs of the Pharisees actually separated them from people even while the Pharisees considered themselves to be perfect or on the way there.

Tradition can come in handy in our desire for self-justification. It can be convenient for dividing the good people from the bad people, with the understanding that the good people make the rules and thereby define *good*.

The underlying problem of tradition that has broken bad is that it ignores the weightier, deeper issues in favor of surface trivia. For all its concern with details, tradition often forgets the importance of flesh-and-blood people. If we forget people and their needs, whatever righteousness we feel is brought to us by our attention to details becomes as worthless and as offensive as filthy rags.

Is our religiousness just a formula or a front, or do we really care about people? Recall that Jesus told a parable about a hurt man, a priest, a Levite, and a despised Samaritan (Luke 10:25-37). The people concerned about tradition failed the test. Have we let this parable teach us to care for people in all our concern for tradition?

Another weighty matter that tradition forgets is the true source of our lives. When tradition dominates our lives, we live on the surface and never dare to dig deeper into our selves. It is easier and safer to follow the rules without facing ourselves.

Proverbs 4:23 reminds us, "Keep your heart with all vigilance, for from it flow the springs of life." How easily we lose ourselves if we do not live from the inside out, if we are content only with surface trivia, and if we allow ourselves to be pushed and pulled and molded by outside traditions alone.

Tradition, for all its surface concern with rightness and wrongness, often ignores the weightiest, most important matter of all—God. Tradition may forget God while claiming to engage in acts that adore God.

The religious leaders of the day had done that. They had become trapped by the idea that they had God safely encased in their tradition. But, in their effort to lock God up, God left. Citing Isaiah 29:13, Jesus said, "Isaiah prophesied rightly about you hypocrites, as it is written, 'This people honors me with their lips, but their hearts are far from me; in vain do they worship me, teaching human precepts as doctrines.' You abandon the commandment of God and hold to human tradition" (Mark 7:6-8).

Let us never think that we have God. Either God has us or we do not have God.

What to Do About Tradition

What are we to do abut tradition, with its values and its faults? We have only one choice as Christians. We must bring whatever traditions we have under the rule of God. We must smash and destroy and leave behind those traditions that are out of harmony with God's will, and we must bring into our hearts only those that are valid and helpful for our day. The prophet Jeremiah spoke of a coming time when God said, "I will put my law within them and I will write it on their hearts; and I will be their God, and they shall be my people" (Jeremiah 31:33). That time is now.

Today we need to ask two questions about our traditions if we would bring them under the will of God and if we would have pure hearts and not just clean hands. First, do our traditions show love for people and encourage us to reach out to them in genuine care? Second, do our traditions lead us to live faithfully from our hearts rather than being content with what is on the surface?

The gospel of the kingdom of God calls and enables us to love God, to be true to our best selves, and to reach out in loving concern to others. It further calls and enables us to bring our longstanding, deeply-embedded traditions and customs under the will of God.

27.
Mark 8:27-38
The Right Place for You
Proper 19 (24):
Sixteenth Sunday after Pentecost

Where is the right place for you? Could it be that lots of folks—even you, even me—are searching for the answer to that question? I believe the answer is *yes, they are* and *yes, we are.*

In fact, people have been looking for the answer since Adam and Eve were expelled from the garden. They have traveled from where they were to where they are now, and they are still traveling, searching for the right place for themselves.

Abram left Ur of the Chaldees to go to Canaan, stopping off in Haran for a while. Later, Moses left Egypt alone, then came back to Egypt, and at last left Egypt for good, leading the Israelites to the entrance to the Promised Land.

Centuries later people from Scandinavia and from Spain left home, searching for the right place. Still later, people from England, France, Spain, Germany, and elsewhere in Europe came to settle in the New World. Others came to the

New World from other places—from Africa, Mexico, Central America, South America, Asia, and all over the world. They were all looking for the right place, or, if they had not come of their own accord, they began looking for it.

In the United States, some moved on from the Eastern seaboard to the West. More recently, some have come from the old home out in the country to the city, looking for the right place. Some stayed home, thinking they had already found it.

Sometimes the search for the right place takes the form of geographical journeying, and sometimes the search is inward. It may well be, as an influential psychologist stated, that below the surface of the lives and problems of people, each person is seeking what we might call this *right place*—our real self.[63] We are looking for that place—within or without—that we feel is *it*— just right for us.

Many of our outward changes of location, vocation, or behavior are rooted in this concern. We all face it. You may be in the middle of life, having already made geographical, vocational, and lifestyle decisions. You may be at the beginning of adult life, wondering what to do with a life stretching out ahead. You may be perhaps at the end of vocational life, but with decisions about living still ahead. Whatever the case, the desire still is to be in the right place.

A *Peanuts* cartoon expressed this desire in a humorous way. Charlie Brown, the insecure little boy who is never in the right place, is talking to

Linus, the wise, also insecure child whose place is wherever his blanket is. Charlie says, "All of us have certain areas in which we feel out of place." Linus responds, "Oh? In what area do *you* feel out of place, Charlie Brown?" With a look of resignation with which many can identify, Charlie replied in one word, "Earth."

Where is the right place for you? How will you know it when you see it? How can you get to it? Is this it? Mark 8:27-38 suggests some answers.

Wrong Answers and a Right One

To know where the right place is, we may need to know first where it is not. Consider three places where the right place is not.

The right place is not necessarily the next place, the next largest place, the next rung on the ladder of success, and not even the last place, the very largest place, or even the very top rung on the tallest ladder of success. It is not necessarily the place of greatest importance and recognition.

The dream of being important, recognized, and successful is powerful in the lives of many people. There's a reason Jesus talked about those who ruled, sought greatness, and desired to exercise authority. Almost every person has this desire, in his or her own way, for importance, for recognition, for success in some way.

The commercials and ads tell us that our dreams are of prestige, honor, popularity, the finest in entertainment and leisure-living, the biggest and best house, the car, the boat, and the vacation trip. We are told we should *have it our*

267

way; that we should *do ourselves a favor*; that we *owe it to ourselves*; that, whatever it is, we *deserve it* today; and that we *need it*.

But the thought that the place of success, recognition, or importance is the right place for us dead-ends at the roadblock of reality. Even the CEO can lose the job; even the multi-millionaire can go bankrupt; even the champion sports figure can find his or her reputation tarnished.

Fame is fleeting. A friend of mine had written several books and had an article published each month in a magazine many people read. He told me once how people would sometimes come up to him and ask, *Didn't you write something sometime?* Sometimes it's so hard to be famous.

The Book of Ecclesiastes deals with this drive for success and recognition. The Teacher says, "Then I considered all that my hands had done and the toil I had spent in doing it, and again, all was vanity and a chasing after wind . . ." (Ecclesiastes 2:11).

A world-famed writer tells of sitting in a restaurant in Paris. He glanced at the other end of the room and saw a particularly miserable-looking man. The man looked familiar. Curiosity got the best of him. He got up to see who it was. He found he was viewing himself in a mirror.

Could that really be how it is—that the right place is not the next place or even the top place? That's what Jesus was telling Peter in this text. Peter was informing Jesus, *Jesus, you've really got it. You're going all the way to the top, and I'll be right with you.* Jesus informed Peter, firmly, even roughly, that his destination was in the other direction entirely. The right place was not the top place, not as people saw it.

Perhaps someone may be saying, *Yes, people ought just to be satisfied with what they have and where they are. Right here is really the right place.* We may think that the right place is right here, in a place of familiarity, comfort, and security.

How easily we get set in our ways, and how tragic when we do. Right here has never been the right place for God's people. Throughout Scripture, God's people were people on a pilgrimage, a divinely-guided journey. The journey may not involve a change in geographical place. It may simply be inward. But it is still a journey.

We are meant to be people who are continually growing, changing, for the better. The person who believes right here is the right place will miss out on life.

People of any age can do this. Young people can get satisfied too soon. They take a little job when they could prepare themselves for one that would mean more to the world and to the cause of Christ. They close themselves off from opportunities. Adults in the middle years can become so in love with security that challenge and risk seem like words in an unfamiliar language. Older adults can refuse to look outward beyond who they are to the growing that they still need to do. It may well be, as someone said, that when we decide we're finished growing, we're finished.

Jesus was teaching Peter that the right place is not right here. Peter had tried to settle down into his own comfortable view of Christ. Christ was the glorious, nationalistic leader. That was a comfortable place, even a desirable place, for Peter, but it was not the right place.

Like Peter, we may feel we left the place of comfort and security a while back. After all, Peter had followed Christ and left his fishing boat. Jesus was now asking him to grow and change again. As with Peter, the reality for us may be that we have now gotten comfortable again. We must beware of becoming too attached to our present comfort and security. It is not the right place for us.

Another place the right place is not is that it is not *nowhere*. Some despair at finding the right place. Like Charlie Brown, they think the right place is not to be found. A lot of people have a lot of despair and hopelessness about life. They feel trapped in hopeless circumstances. Shakespeare portrays that attitude in these lines from *Macbeth*:[64]

> Life's but a walking shadow, a poor player
> That struts and frets his hour upon the
>   stage
> And then is heard no more. It is a tale
> Told by an idiot, full of sound and fury,
> Signifying nothing.

Is that the way it is? Is life a crazy person's dream that means nothing? I admit that that can be the way it sometimes seems. But that's not the way it is. There is a right place for each of us.

Where is it? Where is the right place? The answer is in the text, in verses 33-34. The right place is behind Jesus.

The Greek words *opiso mou* appear in both verses. They mean *behind me.* In verse 33, Jesus commanded Peter, "Get behind me." In verse 34, Jesus actually instructed Peter, *Follow behind me.* That is what Jesus had invited Peter to do when Jesus first called him in Mark 1:17, *Come behind me.* After all, when you follow, don't you have to be behind the person you are following?

Behind Jesus—that is the place where people belong. It is the one right place in all the world. No other place fits. We are restless and out of place if we are not behind Jesus. That is the only place prepared for us. It can be a risky place and a costly place, but it is the only truly right place.

Why Behind Jesus Is the Right Place

Jesus spelled out why behind him is truly the right place in verses 35-38. For one thing, the choice of this place spells the difference between saving our lives and losing our lives. The stakes are high.

Another way of saying the same thing is that only behind Jesus can we make the best bargain for our lives. Where is the profit in gaining the whole world and losing our lives, what we really are and are meant to be? Where is the profit in living life our own way, whatever we think that way is, and then discovering we have lost our true selves or have never really found our true selves?

Behind Jesus is salvation and true life. The Bible proclaims this truth, and experience confirms it.

E. Stanley Jones, the great Methodist Christian leader and missionary, tells how one young person said to a friend the same age, "I'm going to give myself to Jesus Christ. Will you?"

The friend said, "No, I'm going to see life first." They parted and met again thirty years later.

The first said, "Do you remember the night we parted? You said you were going to see life, and I said I was going to see Life, with a capital *L*, Life in Christ. We've had thirty years to test our ways. How did you come out?"

The second person admitted he was dissatisfied, and the first had found satisfaction in Christ. Life behind Jesus, the right place for anyone, had made the difference.[65]

How to Get to the Right Place

Three words stand out in verse 34 to tell us how to get to this right place.

First, deny yourself. That's what Jesus says. The world says, *Eat, drink, and be merry, for tomorrow you die.* Jesus says, *Deny yourself, and live.* Denial and self-discipline seem so antiquated in our day, but to get to the right place requires it.

What does it mean to deny ourselves? It means more than denying things to our selves, although this may be part of it.

To deny self means that we deny first place in our lives to our selves and that we put Jesus there. This decision reaches into our wants and desires, into our hopes and dreams and plans for our lives. We decide to seek to do what God wants instead of what we in our selfishness want. To deny self and put Christ first is not to shove self into oblivion and nothingness. Rather, it is to acknowledge that God wants us at our best and to give ourselves fully to him.

One person tells how he was confused over this conflict to wishing to excel in life and heeding the call of Christ to deny self. Then he saw a motto on the wall of a Christian whom he admired. The motto read, "Make the most of yourself for Christ's sake."[66] That statement helped him know that to excel in one's use of one's gifts and abilities was not in conflict with the call to deny self.

The second thought that stands out in verse 34 is "take up" our cross. The disciples and the early Christians sometimes were faced with the prospect of doing that literally. To be a Christian meant for them to be in danger of death for their faith. Those days have never ended in some parts of the world.

To get yourself into the right place, are you willing to pay the price? Do others recognize you as belonging to the Lord by your lifestyle as well as your words?

The third thought in verse 34 about the way to the right place is "follow me." The old hymn has the line, "Where He leads me, I will follow."[67]

A missionary tells of a Korean woman in a leper colony who attempted to sing that hymn in English. She did well, but in her unfamiliar English it sounded as if she were saying, "Where He *needs* me, I will follow."[68]

Here is an important answer for finding and getting in the right place. Follow the Lord in doing something about the needs you see. You see them because Jesus has led you to see them and may well want you—not someone else—to do something about them. There's a story about a fellow who had the opportunity to ask God a question and receive an answer. He asked why God allowed a certain needy situation, a situation of suffering and difficulty, to go on. God's reply was, *I was just about to ask you that same question.*

So, help the helpless and marginalized in Jesus' name. Do your duty in Jesus' name. Be sensitive to the needs of others in Jesus' name.

Let the needs about you lead you in Christ's service. Serve Jesus in his strength, without complaining, self-pity, or pride. Follow Jesus where he needs you, with the gifts and abilities you have been given.

The novelist and theologian Frederick Buechner has a remarkable sentence worth hearing again and again. It's worth remembering and, more, worth living. It's a sentence that applies well to this matter of finding the right place. Here's what he says: "The place God calls you is the place where your deep gladness and the world's deep hunger meet."[69]

That's the right place for you. It's the place where your deep gladness and the world's deep hunger meet. It's the place behind Jesus. It's true that finding this place calls for self-denial, for taking up your cross, for following Jesus. But it's also a place of great joy, a place where when you look back on your life you can feel you have made a difference.

28.
Mark 10:35-45
A New Standard of Success

Proper 24 (29):
Twenty-First Sunday after Pentecost

Do you think we might have more in common with James and John in this encounter than we will readily admit? It's likely that every person must deal with the desire to be important in some way. Many of us want to be recognized. We at least want to feel others know we exist and matter. We want to be successful, however we define that word.

The ways in which we try to get recognition for ourselves vary. There are many standards of success.

One is monetary, of course. Sometimes we see articles or ads calling us to success. Almost invariably, what they mean is monetary success. The way to be successful in our society has pretty well been set—have a healthy bank account or at least good credit. Or perhaps we measure success by honors and achievements or by the position we have at work, by how many employees report to us.

Let's not kid ourselves. If we don't desire such measurements of success for ourselves, we who have adult children are delighted when they come out well by such measurements, aren't we?

How do such measurements of success relate to what Jesus replied to James and John? After James and John sought from Jesus places of honor and power, Jesus said to them, "You do not know what you are asking" (Mark 10:38). A few exchanges in the conversation later, Jesus continued, "You know that among the Gentiles those whom they recognize as their rulers lord it over them, and their great ones are tyrants over them" (Mark 10:42).

In the case of so many of our standards of success, each is a means of exercising authority in some way. Each of our standards of success can be used to dominate and manipulate others so that they will have to agree that we are important. As in so many other areas, Jesus shows us a better way of looking at such things. He truly gave us a new standard of success.

What's Wrong with the Old Standard of Success?

The text shows us several things that are wrong with the old standard of success. Let me warn you that the old standard of success has such a grip on many of us that we had rather fight than switch. Yet because we will not switch to Jesus' new standard of success, we find life itself to be a constant fight.

Note first that the old standard of success is wrong because of its setting. The Scriptures picture James and John, the sons of Zebedee, coming to Jesus with a request. Likely the request seemed very simple to them. They simply wanted Jesus to do whatever they asked him to do. Jesus would not be trapped, though. He asked James and John to try to be a little more specific, and the truth came out. The two brothers wanted the places of honor and power on the right and left of Jesus.

We may not be as shocked and angered as we should be about the brothers' request since we have heard the story before. The other ten disciples were shocked and angry, though. They were not shocked and angry at the request itself but that James and John had taken the initiative to try to get in front of the line. Only a little earlier, all the disciples had been discussing the question of who was the greatest (9:33-34). The success bug had bitten all of them.

Now, by choosing this text in Mark rather than the parallel passage in Matthew 20:20-28, I have let the mother of these two would-be successes off the hook. But let us not forget that other people often do try by hook and crook to get us to seek success in the old way.

What was the problem with the brothers' request? A big part of the problem was the setting. The setting for this passage in the Gospel of Mark is significant. The disciples had just heard Jesus telling them of his coming death. Jesus had said, "See, we are going up to

Jerusalem, and the Son of Man will be handed over to the chief priests and the scribes, and they will condemn him to death; then they will hand him over to the Gentiles; they will mock him, and spit upon him, and flog him, and kill him; and after three days he will rise again" (Mark 10:33-34). Here Jesus had talked about dying on a cross for the sake of all people. At the same time, the disciples were selfishly trying to figure out how to get ahead in life. They didn't get it, and often neither do we.

The personnel manager of a large corporation said that whenever a young person entered the company's program of executive training, he tried to find out one primary thing about the person. Was the person interested in *being* something or *doing* something? The personnel manager said that the person who simply wanted to *be* something would use the job to make himself or herself look good rather than trying to accomplish something worthwhile.

Isn't this what James and John and even the other ten disciples were doing? They wanted to *be* somebody rather than to accomplish Jesus' mission. They were unwilling to comprehend the *doing* that was going to be required.

A second thing wrong with the old standard of success is the solution. Jesus told James and John, who wanted to be important, "You do not know what you are asking" (Mark 10:38).

What was the problem with their request? For one thing, the highest degree of success calls for still another achievement, still another dollar, still another rung on the ladder. When we try to be successful in the way the world counts success, we are putting ourselves on an endless treadmill.

The story is told of Alexander the Great that after conquering much of the known world of his day he wept because, he said, there were not other worlds to conquer. He wanted and needed more.

One of the richest people in the world was asked how much wealth was required for a person to be satisfied. He revealed his own standard of success when he replied, "Only a little more."

When we crave success by the old standard, the standard James and John used, we know not what we are asking. There will always be something lacking.

The solution of the old standard of success is wrong for another reason. What do we do when we fail? Does that mean you are not important, that you are worthless? It's easy to feel that way.

When I was in seminary, I served as a professor's assistant, grading undergraduate student papers. I think I was kind, but I recall one young person who was very concerned when he did not get a top grade. He felt, he said, that this meant that he was not a very good person. His image of himself was threatened when he did not get a top grade. He thought he was a failure as a person.

There's a third thing wrong with the old standard of success, and that is the kind of society the old standard creates. The old standard of success creates a society in which people are suspicious of others, envious of others, angry with others. "When the ten heard it, they began to be angry with James and John," says Mark 10:41. Why were they angry? They were angry because they felt that the two brothers were trying to get ahead of the rest of them.

If the Twelve were a basketball team, right about then they would have started a long losing streak. There may be stars on a basketball team, but if they do not submit their individual talents to the good of the team, they likely will lose some games they should have won. In the disciples' case, they weren't paying attention to the coach.

Someone has pointed out that one of the problems of American culture is that so many people are trying so dreadfully hard to impress others so that they can get somebody to say that they are worth something, that they are important. We often try to sell ourselves to others, like an advertiser trying to sell toothpaste. We look around to see what people are buying in people, and we dress ourselves up to fit that image. Actually there are seminars and books that teach this. Even so, in the process, we lose ourselves—our own unique, God-given individuality and our own sense of worth. We sell ourselves out, like Esau did to Jacob in the Book of Genesis, all for a mess of pottage.

I once heard Jim Collins, the brilliant author of the influential business book *Good to Great*, say that comparison is our secular sin. That is, businesses compare themselves to other businesses rather than seeking to become the best they can become by offering the best services and products of which they are capable for their customers. The disciples were comparing themselves to one another rather than focusing on what their Leader was doing and wanted each of them to do.

Jesus' New Standard of Success

Notice how different Jesus' new standard of success is. Jesus said, "Whoever wishes to become great among you must be your servant, and whoever wishes to be first among you must be slave of all" (Mark 10:43-44). Jesus calls us to cast aside our definitions of success, our desire for others' approval, our greed for a little niche or a big corner for ourselves.

Do I have to tell you this is not easy for most of us, if not all of us? The fact is that every muscle, bone, and cell within us cries out against our doing this. Honestly, when it comes to living life, don't we feel more comfortable with James and John and the angry disciples than we do with Jesus? Don't we feel that status *is* important, that recognition *is* important, that being important *is* important?

Plus, we are not very keen on this servant thing. Being a servant seems beneath us. We forget that Jesus was the only perfect human being and he was a servant. But we still prefer being important to being a servant.

Look, though, at the advantage of being a servant. What does this new way of success offer?

It frees us to live positively. When we become servants, people who are willing to be last, something good happens. We stop trying to figure out ways to get recognition and start trying to find ways to help. We stop trying to use our job, our family, and our friends in order to make ourselves look good. We start trying to be people who care about others.

Then something else happens. We discover deep within that we are already a success and we do not have to strive to be successful. Here are some wise words from one commentator on this passage: "If we have been called, appointed to be saints, made a part of Christ's Body, what more do we need? We have been made great; why struggle for greatness?"[70] We do not have to strive to be important. In and through Christ, we already are.

With Nicodemus in John 3, we may be asking of Jesus, *How can this be?* How can a person be a servant and still be a success?

It works like this. Our whole idea about ourselves is that we aren't worth anything until we achieve and acquire and then get someone else to say we're a success. Jesus' new standard of success says that because we are children of God, we are worth something to begin with. We are important because God says we are important. God's great love for us makes us important.

This idea is liberating if we can ever get hold of it and get it into our lives. Until we do, though, we may be Christians and still feel guilty, inadequate, burdened, and driven by the world's old standard of success. We may not really be willing to be servants, people who live and care for others. We are all susceptible to this, but we don't have to stay like this.

Sam Shoemaker (1893-1963) was an Episcopal priest who assisted in establishing Alcoholics Anonymous. He said, "The people who let themselves be loved by God are the people who can accept themselves, and then give themselves away in love to their neighbors."[71]

That fits well with what the passage in Mark is saying about Jesus' new standard of success. Let us become people who know they are loved by God and can thus give ourselves away in love to others, for Jesus' sake.

29.
Job 42:1-6, 10-17
A Problem for Faith

Proper 25 (30):
Twenty-Second Sunday after Pentecost

The Book of Job is part of the lore of Western culture, not just a book in the Bible. That being the case, almost every one knows the story, or at least some part of it.

To summarize, though, Job had everything. He was personally upright, even blameless. He was in good health. He had a fine family. He had many possessions. He had much respect. He was living the dream of just about everybody. He even served God. He served God because he loved God, not for what he could get out of it.

Yet, only a step past the beginning of the story, through the actions of Satan with the permission of God, Job lost everything except his life. He lost his family, he lost his possessions, he lost his status, he lost his health. Well, he did have four more things he didn't lose. He had four guys who claimed to be his friends. With friends like those, though, Job didn't need any enemies.

So Job had lost pretty much everything. He was a man in suffering, and that was a grave

287

problem even beyond the suffering itself. The notion in that time was that if someone was hurting in some way, the reason was sin. Job's so-called friends tried over and over to convince Job of that. Each friend in his own way tried to say to Job, *Cheer up, brother. It's all your fault. You've sinned; you know you have. And that's why all these bad things have happened to you.*

Job couldn't figure out why all those bad things had happened to him, though. He did not know the why of his suffering. He knew, however, that he had done nothing to bring it on—not even sin. He was not saying he was perfect. What he was saying was that how he had lived and what had happened to him did not match up, not even remotely.

Certainly the Book of Job is about suffering. It is also about other things as well. The book by and by explores much of the whole range of a person's relationship to God. It explores the nature of faith and doubt, and it explores both God's nearness and God's distance.

Job's Problem: How Can I Get to God?

Throughout the book, Job voiced a big problem he was having. *How can I get to God? Here I am suffering greatly from the loss of so much that I cherished, plus having to endure cruel accusations from my so-called friends. Where is God? Doesn't God care?*

Listen to Job crying out to God. "O that I might have my request, and that God would grant my desire" (Job 6:8). "Look, he passes by me, and

I do not see him; he moves on, but I do not perceive him" (9:11). "Do not condemn me; let me know why you contend against me" (10:2). "Why do you hide your face, and count me as your enemy?" (13:24). "Oh, that I knew where I might find him, that I might come even to his dwelling" (23:3). "If I go forward, he is not there; or backward, I cannot perceive him; on the left he hides, and I cannot behold him; I turn to the right, but I cannot see him" (23:8-9). "O that I were as in the months of old, as in the days when God watched over me; when his lamp shown over my head, and by his light I walked through darkness; when I was in my prime . . ." (29:2-4a). "I cry to you and you do not answer me; I stand, and you merely look at me. You have turned cruel to me . . ." (30:20-21a).

For Job, God seemed very far away. He would never have said he did not believe in God. He lived in a culture that believed in God, sometimes many gods. Not to believe in God was simply not the done thing. But that may well be how Job would have expressed his feelings today. The problem of suffering is one of the big barriers to belief in God.

However we express it ourselves, who among us does not know what Job is talking about? So many have felt at one time or another, for one reason or another, that God is far away, that we cannot get to God. Perhaps we have been tempted to stop believing in God at all. Perhaps some of us have.

Things go along well enough in regular times, ordinary times. But in quiet moments, or when a crisis strikes, we realize that God seems far away and that we somehow cannot get to God. Job's problem is our problem.

How Did It Happen?

How did Job get to this point? How did it happen that God seemed so far away and unresponsive and perhaps, as we might say, not even exist? Of course, it all began with Job's experiences of loss. But it continued with more, much more.

Right off we should respond to the question by saying that Job's utter frustration with his suffering plus the condemnation from his friends could easily have led him to this feeling of being out of touch with God. Job felt he had been done a great injustice. He had been faithful, and yet he was suffering. His friends were using the theology of the day to accuse him of sin, and the evidence for the charge was that he was suffering. There— quite easily done, to their way of thinking.

Job was getting no help from his friends or from God, and Job was utterly frustrated by it all. God seemed so far away in the midst of his difficulties.

Another thing could have led Job to feeling God was distant and unresponsive. That other thing was Job himself. As the Book of Job progresses, Job gets more and more strident in his complaints. About three-fourths of the way through the long Book of Job, we find Job issuing a rebellious, prideful challenge to God. Job complained, "O that I had one to hear me! (Here is my signature! Let the Almighty answer me!) O that I had the indictment written by my adversary! Surely I would carry it on my shoulder; I would bind it on me like a crown; I would give him an account of all my steps; like a prince I would approach him" (31:35-37).

Perhaps Job was so intent on proving himself to be right that he forgot that human beings can hardly be prideful before God. Yet Job challenged God.

What does this say to us? Let us beware of stifling honest doubt and inquiry. Frankly, there are as many arguments, and as strong, for God's existence as against, or against as for. Our belief, or lack, is a matter of faith, personal decision, an act of will, an act of commitment. We do "pay our money and take our choice." More about that in a moment. For now, let us just say that we should not stifle honest doubt and inquiry. Jesus didn't. Remember Thomas, the disciple we call Doubting Thomas? Even so, is it possible that some of the arguments against God are rooted simply in the desire to have our own way? It is more convenient to push God into a corner—out of sight, out of mind—in order to do our own thing.

For us as for Job, God may seem very far away. Circumstances may have pushed him away and closed our eyes to him. Or we may have sent God away ourselves through own pride and rebelliousness.

What to Do? How to Respond?

Whatever the reasons for Job's feelings that God was distant and uncaring, we can rejoice that it did not remain that way with him. Out of the whirlwind God spoke to Job.

God asked Job countless questions Job could not answer. God's questioning Job in chapters 38 through 41 was a dramatic way of reminding Job of his weakness and God's greatness. We find Job saying, in essence, *I spoke foolishly, Lord. What can I answer? I see my smallness and your greatness. I will not try to say anything else. I have already said more than I should* (40:3-5). In our text, Job said to God, *I know that you are all-powerful, that you can do anything you want. Before this, I knew only what others had told me, but now I have seen and heard you. So I am ashamed of all I have said* (42:1-6).

Job had felt God was distant from him. Then, at the end of the book, Job knew God wasn't distant but near. Job had longed for God, called for God, prayed for God, and challenged God. At the end of the book, Job knew God was near.

God responded to Job in a way that utterly surprised him. Job had thought he would haughtily present his case before God and make God explain what had happened. That's not what occurred, though. When God responded to Job, God didn't so much give answers to Job's questions and challenges as offer assurance to Job of his nearness.

Frankly, the Book of Job doesn't give answers to us, either. The book tantalizes us to think about the problem of our suffering and to learn that there are no easy answers. That's the big message of Job, in fact.

Job's friends represented the theologians of his day who had it all figured out. God rebuked them at the end of the book. God both rebuked and commended Job at the end of the book, too. Job got his health and wealth restored, and he got a fresh start with a new family, too. Of course, we know that doesn't nearly always happen in real life. We know that people get sick and sometimes get well and sometimes not. We know that we never get over losing loved ones. We may adjust and move through the experience, but there's still a void. That's what friends of mine who have lost children tell me, too.

Great public tragedies seem to occur over and over these days. After every single tragedy, the question that is always discussed is, *Why did God let this happen?* In almost every case, the most important thing is not a logical answer to this question but a reminder that our loving God cares and is present.

Like you, I wish I had all the answers. When it comes down to it, though, I am most glad to get a sense of a loving God's near presence.

Look at what happened in Job's faith as the book concludes. One thing is that Job acknowledged God's greatness. Couldn't we live with more assurance about life if we were more aware of God's greatness? A second thing, the greatest thing, is that Job became acutely aware of God's presence and nearness. Rather than answers, I believe that's what we want, too.

G. A. Studdert-Kennedy (1883-1929) was an Anglican priest, a chaplain in World War I, and an author of poems and other writings that articulated the Christian faith. In his poem titled "Faith," he points up the problem of faith Job faced and that we face, plus the only way of solving the problem. Here's a part of that poem:

How do I know that God is good? I don't.
I gamble like a man. I bet my life upon one
    side
in life's great war. I must, I can't stand out.
I must take sides.
....
How is it proved? It isn't proved, you fool; it
can't be proved.
....
I know not why the Evil,
I know not why the Good,
both mysteries remain unsolved and both
    insoluble.

I know that both are there, the battle set,
and I must fight on this side or on that.
I can't stand shivering on the bank, I
plunge head first.
....
Such is my Faith, and such
my reasons for it, and I find them strong
    enough.

And you? You want to argue? Well, I can't.
It's a choice. And I choose Christ.[72]

30.
Mark 12:28-34
Where It All Begins

Proper 26 (31):
Twenty-Third Sunday after Pentecost

Time magazine named Albert Einstein the person of the century for the twentieth century.[73] He's most famous, of course, for his "theory of relativity," which has revolutionized much of the scientific world.

Now, it's not the purpose of this meditation to explain the theory of relativity to you just now, and so I won't. I will say, though, that one of the best definitions of the theory of relativity I've come across is the one I heard Garrison Keillor offer in the long-running radio show, *Prairie Home Companion*. He said that the theory of relativity says that the longer you are around your relatives the slower time passes. Probably that's not what Einstein had in mind.

What Einstein really said that I want to point you to, though, is this statement, which is one of his more well-known quotes: "Confusion of goals and perfection of means seems, in my opinion, to characterize our age." That is, we have perfected the means to do many things, but our goals are muddled. We are technologically capable of doing many things; we know the processes. However, we don't have much of an idea about why we're doing them or the goals toward which we are putting this technology to work. We have marvelous means for living life—like the mechanical gadgets that make our work much less difficult, like modern means of transportation and communication, like more to choose from when we want to buy something. The problem, though, is that we do not know quite why we have it and what is the best purpose for it.

Having excellent means without a clear idea of the best use to which to put them leads to foolish if not destructive behavior. We need to know where we're going, with a clear focus on what is important.

That's where it all begins, and that's where Jesus began in his response to the scribe who came asking, "Which commandment is the first of all?" (Mark 12:28). The scribe had come asking Jesus about the commandment that was first of all because he was seeking this place where it all begins. It was traditional to say that there were 613 individual laws that needed to be followed if one kept the whole law. The rabbis had often made attempts to summarize these 613 commandments into one or two brief statements.

The scribe wanted to know how Jesus would summarize the law. Jesus gave the answer and in so doing pointed the scribe and us to the place where it all begins. Notice again what Jesus said.

Love God

Jesus said first that we are to have a genuine and all-encompassing love for God. Jesus pointed back to the *shema*, which the pious scribe and indeed all pious Jews would say every day. Jesus said that the first commandment, the most important one, is this: "Hear, O Israel: the Lord our God, the Lord is one; you shall love the Lord your God with all your heart, and with all your soul, and with all your mind, and with all your strength." These words are straight out of the Old Testament, from Deuteronomy 6:4-5.

There is one God, Jesus was saying, and this God deserves all your love. A genuine love for God is a key to the place where it all begins in life.

But what does it mean to "love the Lord your God"? Two words come to mind.

The first is gratitude. Loving the Lord our God means showing gratitude to God. One wonders how well we do that. Just a few verses following the passage Jesus quoted from Deuteronomy, the Hebrews were commanded not to forget God when they began to live in the place of blessing to which they were going. They were not to forget God when they entered "a land with fine, large cities that you did not build, houses filled with all sorts of goods that you did not fill, hewn cisterns that you did not hew, vineyards and olive groves that you did not plant" (Deuteronomy 6:10-11).

But they forgot. And so do we. We assume all too readily that what we have we deserve if not more. One generation believes they deserve it because they worked for it. Another believes they deserve it because they have always had it and are thereby entitled to it for some unknown reason. But both generations treat lightly God's role in providing them the blessings they have.

Preachers and laypeople alike used to tell the shabby little story of the man saying to a gardener or farmer, "What a wonderful garden—or farm—you and God made." The gardener replies, "Yes, but you should have seen it when God had it alone." And there is some humor in that, but not much. I would like to see it when the man had it alone—with no sun and no rain and no air and no seasons and no seeds and no fertile ground. All that we use and so proudly call *ours* and *mine* is in fact only entrusted to us and not given. Loving God means living in gratitude to God.

There's a second word that helps us understand the meaning of "love the Lord your God." It's not a popular word today even in the midst of all the talk about God and spirituality. There's a good bit of interest in spiritual things in some circles these days, but this word sometimes gets left out. It's the word faithfulness. Loving God means being faithful to God, even obeying God.

Jesus said to his disciples on the last night of his earthly life, "If you love me, you will keep my commandments" (John 14:15). Obeying God is a part of loving God.

Loving God means living in gratitude to God and being obedient to God. Doing this in a halfway manner won't do. We are to love God in these ways with all our heart, soul, mind, and strength—with all of ourselves, in other words.

Just a few verses down from our text is the story of the poor widow (Mark 12:41-44). Out of gratitude to God and obedience to God, she put into the temple treasury "everything she had, all she had to live on" (12:44). That's the meaning of loving God with all our heart, soul, mind, and strength. We give all of ourselves, not just a part, and not just a large part—but all.

I wish I could tell how to do this in *1-2-3*-step manner. I can tell you that it's all about focus, all about recognizing what is important and going that way regardless of what culture and other people say. For many of us, it's only when the years mount up that we recognize that so many of the ambitions, so many of the arguments, so much of the complaining, so much of the wanting, and so much of the grasping for things weren't worth it. Such things really weren't important, and we missed so much of what *was* important.

When we gathered to celebrate my father's eighty-ninth birthday, we knew he was growing steadily weaker from cancer. None of us knew for sure, of course, whether he might live months or years or, as it turned out, weeks. It was at once a somber occasion and a delightful, happy one.

After we had enjoyed a family dinner plus birthday cake and ice cream and after most of the other family members had left, I announced that I was going to mow the yard. It was May, the grass was high, and I thought of mowing the yard as my responsibility during my visits. Too, since I lived several hundred miles away, I felt my time was limited. Imagine that.

Daddy, though, knowing of his weakening condition and recognizing that his time truly *was* limited, went to the heart of what was important. With characteristic directness, he said, "Let the grass go. Sit here and visit." His words did not seem so insightful at the time. After all, I felt *I* had only a little time, and the grass was getting too high. But his worsened condition only a few weeks later made clear the wisdom of his words. They went to the heart of what was—and is— important. "Let the grass go. Sit here and visit."

Along those lines, humorist and now Senator Al Franken once said that he was raised in the time before quality time. Therefore, his parents just spent quantity time with him. This may sound like I've gotten off track, but I haven't. Loving God with our whole hearts and lives means focusing on what's really important. Furthermore, it means loving God in the small ways of daily life as well as in the larger ways.

Love People

Jesus said a second place was where it all begins, too. We are to love God fully. We are also to love people. We are to love our neighbors as we love ourselves.

When Jesus answered the scribe's question, he joined the command to love God fully with the command to love our neighbors as ourselves. It, too, was straight from the Old Testament, in Leviticus 19:18.

"Love your neighbor as yourself" (Mark 12:31). It's simple to say, but it won't be any easier to do tomorrow than it was yesterday, most likely. Why?

Neighbors seem to call for our care at some of the most inconvenient times and in some of the most inconvenient ways. This business of love for other people is difficult because it calls us to go out of our way to do what we need to do and not just what we want to do.

Loving our neighbors as ourselves is difficult for another reason, too. Some people just aren't the best neighbors. They aren't "our kind of people." They're still our neighbors, though.

Jesus said, "Whoever wants to be first must be last of all and servant of all" (Mark 9:35). Do you know the one word in that verse that is the most problem to us? It's the word "all." We are willing to love and serve some people, some neighbors—most if not all of our family, our friends, our friends' families, our class, our race. To love and serve "all" is the hardest part.

We live in a multicultural society and a multicultural world. Christians need to lead the way and not drag along behind government in showing love to all people. It is tragic that many Christians and many churches continue to be known as people who discriminate even as white churches were known during the days of the civil rights struggle in the latter half of the twentieth century.

Sometimes we think it would be easier to love our neighbors, all of them, if we just had better neighbors. We think the problem is the kind of neighbors we have. Actually, as Jesus said in his parable of the Good Samaritan, the problem and the answer is in the kind of neighbors we *are*. The question Jesus leaves us with in that parable is, who "was a neighbor to the man who fell into the hands of the robbers?" (Luke 10:36). The relevant question is not, "Who is my neighbor?" but *Am I a good neighbor?* That is, do I love my neighbor as myself?

How do we know whether someone loves God anyway? by how much they talk about God? by how many songs they sing about God? by how holy they look? Of course not. The proof of our love for God is in our love for our fellow human beings. As 1 John 4:20 says so clearly, "Those who say, 'I love God,' and hate their brothers or sisters, are liars; for those who do not love a brother or sister whom they have seen, cannot love God whom they have not seen."

Someone has said that we love God only as much as we love the human being whom we love the least. Don't you hope that's not right? Aren't you afraid that it is?

A woman who became a Christian late in life said that the simple acts of love shown her by another Christian told her that the love of the God the Bible talked about was really real. There really is no other way than the way of love for God and love for other people.

Loving God with our whole lives and loving our neighbors as ourselves—that's where it all begins. I guess I could try to make this more complicated, but it's not rocket science. It's really where it all begins, or it doesn't begin at all very well and it doesn't go anywhere we want to go. It's where it ends, too.

There's an interesting conclusion to the encounter in this passage that we sometimes miss. Verse 34 says, "After that no one dared to ask him any question." They were silent. What Jesus had said was so plain. They understood it well. They were like children with their hands caught in the cookie jar or like adults before God's judgment bar.

What could they say? They were silent. What could they do about it? They could surrender themselves to Jesus of Nazareth, to do what Jesus and the age-old teachings said to do—love God with all our heart, soul, mind, and strength, and love our neighbors as ourselves. We could do that, too if we wanted to, right now. Why don't we?

So reach out to God and reach over to your neighbor, in love. That's where it all begins.

31.
Hebrews 9:24-28
Can Things Ever Be All Right Again?

Proper 27 (32):
Twenty-Fourth Sunday after Pentecost

Let's begin by talking about something that is common to a good many if not all of us in one way or another. We do have different viewpoints on it, though, depending on where we are in our life situation. The something we have in common is the troubles and difficulties of life.

One person put it this way for a certain age bracket. He said,

> If you look at any man or woman fifty years of age or more, you will see on their face a reflection of struggle and trouble. The women can cover it up a little better with the help of the beauty parlor but every person who has lived a half-century knows that the main characteristic of their existence has been problems and difficulties. Indeed, if I were the President of the United States, I would give every person fifty years of age who is still out of jail a purple heart.[74]

Is it really that bad? I'm sure I've been fortunate in comparison to some people, but having lived well past that fateful age, it doesn't seem that bad. Maybe that person who said it—a preacher in a sermon—just got up on the wrong side of the bed the Sunday morning he said those words.

Perhaps, too, he was putting a little too much emphasis on a certain age bracket. G. K. Chesterton, the British writer of the early twentieth century (1874-1936), balanced things out a bit as he took issue with those folks who say that youth is a time of happiness and hope and beyond that, all that remains is trouble and despair. He said that for youth, "The end of every episode is the end of the world. But the power of hoping through everything, the knowledge that the soul survives its adventures, that great inspiration comes to the middle-aged."[75]

Well, maybe. It's always dangerous to generalize. Every generalization runs the danger of being false, including this one.

I actually think that what both of these folks said has truth in it. There are troubles and difficulties for people of every age bracket— young, middle-aged, old, really old, and old-as-the-hills old. You decide which age bracket is yours. But when we ourselves are at our worst— when *we* have gotten up on the wrong side of the bed or when some terrible tragedy has hit us— then it is that we all, young or not-so-young anymore, are looking for and hoping for something better. Then it is that we all likely start asking ourselves, *Can things ever be all right again?*

Well, can they? We need the hope that they can. We have a saying, sometimes spoken in hushed tones in hospital waiting rooms, "Where there's life, there's hope." Where a thread of life remains, we often feel that something can be done, whether it actually can or not.

But the reverse of that statement is also true, perhaps even truer. "Where there's hope, there's life." We need hope, else we cannot truly live.

How much hope do you have? Do you think that things can ever be all right again? It may be hard to say about the specific troubles and difficulties with which we are dealing today. However, concerning the big picture of life and of our lives, this Scripture passage gives us a clear *yes*. Let's explore that *yes*.

This passage and the gospel as a whole say, *Yes, things can be all right again.* They affirm this on the basis of the three appearings of Christ that are portrayed in this text. In this passage, the writer of Hebrews spoke of not one, not two, but three appearings of Christ. Each appearance tells us a way in which Christ brings us hope even as we face trouble and difficulties.[76]

Christ's First Appearing

The passage says we can have hope that things will be all right again because of Christ's first appearing. This first appearing is Jesus' historical life. This appearing is what the writer to the Hebrews had in mind when he wrote about

307

Christ, "But as it is, he has appeared once for all at the end of the age to remove sin by the sacrifice of himself" (Hebrews 9:26). This first appearing of Christ, when he came to "remove sin by the sacrifice of himself," brings us hope. It says to us, *Yes, things can be all right again.*

The Book of Hebrews emphasizes strongly the truth that the most important thing in life is having access to God. Scripture here and elsewhere teaches that the most important thing in life is being in tune with God, being able to approach and relate to God.

The message of the New Testament is that there are things that last and things that don't. There are things worth living for and even dying for, and there are things that are trivial in comparison. A person's relationship to God fits in the first category. It lasts, it is worth living for, and it is even worth dying for. It is the most important thing in life, in fact.

But there is a problem. Our sin, our departure from God's purposes, from God's way, has blocked the way to God. To the extent that things are that way in your life and you cannot get to God, you lack hope. If you, as Paul says, are "without God in the world," you lack hope (Ephesians 2:12).

In Jesus' first appearing, he came to do something about our hopeless condition. He came to bring us hope. He came to open up the way to God. Even more, he came to *be* that way (John 14:6). Thanks to Jesus and what Jesus did in his first appearing, we have access to God, and we have hope.

At the cross, Jesus offered himself for our sins. He showed people once and for all, unmistakably, vividly, that God loves us and receives us in spite of our sin. He showed us once and for all the extent of God's love for us. One of the great summary verses of Scripture about God and our relationship with God is this: "God proves his love for us in that while we still were sinners Christ died for us" (Romans 5:8).

If God cares this much for us, shouldn't we have hope? Shouldn't we know that, yes, things can be all right again? And when we experience the forgiveness of sin, the lifting of the burdens and penalties of sin, doesn't this give us hope?

The poet Louisa Fletcher wished for a "land of beginning again." She wrote,[77]

> I wish that there were some wonderful
>   place
> In the Land of Beginning Again.
> Where all our mistakes and all our
>   heartaches
> And all of our poor selfish grief
> Could be dropped like a shabby old coat at
>   the door
> and never put on again.

The first appearing of Christ, when he came to "remove sin by the sacrifice of himself" (Heb. 9:26), tells us that there is such a place. It is the place where we meet Christ in repentance and faith and receive his forgiveness. This gives us hope, and we know that things indeed can be all right again.

Christ's Present Appearing

We can find hope also in Christ's present appearing, in what Christ is doing right now and where Christ is right now. Where is Christ appearing right now?

You remember, of course, that great promise of Jesus in what we call the Great Commission. What did Jesus say about where he is right now? He said, "Remember, I am with you always" (Matthew 28:20). That's where Jesus is right now. He is with us. This is a tremendous source of hope, a great assurance that things can be all right again. Jesus is with us. He is present with us in the Spirit.

The writer of Hebrews wouldn't argue with this, I'm sure. But he would also say something else. In fact, he did say it. He said that Christ is somewhere else, too. Christ is appearing somewhere else at the same time, now, in the present. Hebrews says that Christ has "entered into heaven itself, now to appear in the presence of God on our behalf" (Heb. 9:24).

Where is Christ now? Christ now appears in the presence of God on our behalf.

So things are not hopeless. We are not separated from God, distant from God. Do you remember the old gospel song, "What a Friend We Have in Jesus"?[78] Jesus, our Friend, is there in heaven itself, in the very presence of God. Why is Jesus there? What is Jesus doing there? Jesus, our Friend, is there "on our behalf." He is taking our confessions of sins, our concerns, our deepest problems, and our griefs, and he is laying them out before God for a loving, powerful God to deal with.

Jesus is not only with us, but he is also with God, sharing with God our concerns and interceding for us. Doesn't this bring hope? Christ appears now in the presence of God "on our behalf." How can things help but be all right again in some way? We can have hope.

Christ's Coming Appearing

When things seem hopeless, we can find hope in yet another appearing of Christ. Hebrews says, "Christ, having been offered once to bear the sins of many, will appear a second time, not to deal with sin, but to save those who are eagerly waiting for him" (9:28). Jesus' appearance at what we call his Second Coming brings us hope. We often ask, *Can things ever be all right again?* The answer is a loud, confident *yes!*

There are many questions about the details of the Second Coming. Some folks feel they have the answers about all the details, and they generally are very glad to tell whomever they can get to listen. Sometimes they even want to argue with and break fellowship with anyone who disagrees with them about the details.

Rather than focus on the details, though, let's focus on the meaning. Jesus' promised appearing that is still to come, Jesus' Second Coming, means hope. Pure and simple, that's what it means. To some folks, this talk about Jesus' Second Coming is cause for anxiety and fear. Really, though, at its heart, the Second Coming is a stimulus for Christian living and a cause for hope.

Jesus' Second Coming will mean victory. When our Christian brothers and sisters of the first century were being persecuted, surely they found great encouragement in the truth that although things looked very dark, Jesus was going to be victorious. This is the message that the Book of Revelation proclaimed to them and that it proclaims to us now. Things may not be easy now, but there will come a day when

> The kingdom of the world has become the
> kingdom of our Lord
> and of his Messiah,
> and he will reign forever and ever
> (Revelation 11:15).

Further, Jesus' Second Coming will bring to us salvation in its fullness. No matter where you are in your Christian life, you are not as saved today as one day you will be. There is more to come. God wants to make us more and more like Jesus. God wants to bring salvation in its fullness to us, and God will do this completely at Jesus' Second Coming. This truth gives us hope.

Moreover, Jesus' coming again will indeed make everything all right again. Do you remember when you were a child and you fell and skinned your knee? Perhaps you went to Mom or Dad or someone else special and said, "Make it better. Make it well." That is our concern today as we struggle with difficulty, tragedy, and loss. We want things to be all right again.

Things will be all right as we trust in God. As another passage in Revelation reminds us,

Then I saw a new heaven and a new earth; for the first heaven and the first earth had passed away, and the sea was no more. And I saw the holy city, the new Jerusalem, coming down out of heaven from God, prepared as a bride adorned for her husband.

And I heard a loud voice from the throne saying,

"See, the home of God is among
   mortals.
He will dwell with them as their
   God;
they will be his peoples,
and God himself will be with them;
he will wipe every tear from their
   eyes.
Death will be no more;
mourning and crying and pain will
   be no more,
for the first things have passed
   away."

And the one who was seated on the throne said, "See, I am making all things new" (Rev. 21:1-5).

God will "make it better," as the little child asked. Of that we can be sure. It may not be as it was before we experienced the difficulty, but God will make it better.

We may feel we have a lot of bad things to face. We may even feel as if all hope is lost. But the first appearing of Christ—his coming to live among people in his earthly life—and the second appearing of Christ—his intercession with God on our behalf—and the coming appearing of Christ all assure us that hope is not lost. As Paul wrote, "If God is for us, who is against us?" (Romans 8:31).

32.
1 Kings 17:1-16
Open to the Unusual
Proper 27 (32):
Twenty-Fourth Sunday after Pentecost

Researchers have suggested that every time we think an idea, we form a little furrow in our brain.[79] If we keep on thinking that idea and don't allow ourselves to consider other ideas, that shallow furrow becomes a deeper and deeper rut.[80] Do you know anyone whose brain evidently has deep ruts in it, so deep that he or she can't see a new idea, respond in a new way to a challenge, or act in a new way?

Of course, holding to a tried-and-true idea or taking a familiar action can be good if the thought or behavior is a good one and continues to be the most appropriate response. However, responding in such familiar ways may limit us unnecessarily and even be disastrous when a higher, better response is called for. In this passage of Scripture, we see a couple of people considering and then practicing an unusual way of responding rather than relying on the familiar.

There are lots of big challenges in our world and in our lives. These challenges may call us to respond in new, unusual, large, challenging, even risky ways if we are to follow God's instructions. How will we respond?

Unusual Instructions, Divine Provision (17:1-7)

Verse 1 begins the story of the prophet Elijah, which runs through 2 Kings 2. It also begins to highlight the story of God's prophets versus the kings of Israel who were not faithful to God. That is the story of much of the rest of 1 and 2 Kings.

This verse provides much information about who Elijah was and about his historical setting. Even Elijah's name indicates who he was. His name combines forms of Eli, a divine name (*El*), and Yahweh, the covenant name of God (*Yah*). Thus Elijah's name itself means that Yahweh was his God.[81] In Elijah's later actions he would live up to his name. No one who knew Elijah would doubt who his God was.

Elijah was from Gilead in the Northern kingdom (also called Israel). The region of Gilead, where the tribe of Gilead had settled centuries earlier, was located on the east side of the Jordan River. Tishbe may refer to a village, the location of which is unknown, or it may instead mean *settler.*

Elijah prophesied during the reign of King Ahab of Israel (869-850 BC). Thus, Elijah's time is roughly fifty to seventy-five years after the Northern and Southern kingdoms had split under Rehoboam in 922 B.C.

The times had not been pleasant for Israel since the split. In fact, the times had been wild and unstable, permeated by political intrigue and further falling away from the worship of Yahweh.

King Ahab had come to power through succeeding his father, Omri. Omri was a strong king but one who "did what was evil in the sight of the Lord" (1 Kings 16:25).

King Ahab and his wife Jezebel had not helped the nation's troubling situation. Jezebel was from Phoenicia and was a worshiper of Baal. With Jezebel's strong encouragement, her husband Ahab had promoted Baal worship rather than the worship of the true God.

Enter Elijah. Even in this one verse, we can tell that Elijah and Ahab would not get along well. No rain or dew, said Elijah, for three years, not unless I say so. Imagine a mere prophet saying that to a mighty king.

Our common idea about prophets is that they predict the future. There was some of that in the work of the prophets. Mainly, though, the prophets were messengers from God. They were to listen to God and convey God's message although that message might not meet majority approval or the approval of the ruler at the time. From here on, especially through the time of the Exile, first of the Northern kingdom and then of the Southern kingdom, God's prophets would play a major role in confronting Israel and its leaders with their need to follow God.

Rain generally came seasonally from October to March, and heavy dew that seemed almost like a drizzle occurred in the higher elevations during the hot season.[82] Elijah's word about no rain challenged the king's ability to bring prosperity to his subjects. Not only that, Elijah's word also challenged Ahab and Jezebel's god Baal. Baal was the storm god, the god of the rain. Baal was supposed to bring fertility to crops and animals. With no rain, there would be no fertility.

The action in verses 2-7 occurs east of the Jordan at a place called the Wadi Cherith. "Wadi" means brook, ravine, or creek. The Wadi Cherith would provide water for Elijah. So for a time there would be enough water in the east for Elijah to survive, but there would not be rain in the west, where King Ahab was.

In addition to water, God also provided food for Elijah. At the Lord's command, ravens brought Elijah "bread and meat" in the morning and in the evening (17:6). Even for a prophet, ravens would have been an unusual way of getting food, since ravens eat carrion.

More Unusual Instructions, More Divine Provision (17:8-16)

After the brook dried up and no water was available for Elijah, God still provided for him. Again God did this in an unusual manner. God sent Elijah to the village of Zarephath in Sidon. The region of Sidon hugged the Mediterranean coast, far to the northwest from Israel. Zarephath was located in this distant region between the cities of Tyre and Sidon.

A significant fact about the location of Zarephath is that the village was in the heart of the pagan god Baal's home country. Nevertheless, God would provide for Elijah there.

How God provided for Elijah was again unusual. Note the irony. To provide for Elijah during the drought and famine, God sent Elijah to a poor widow who had only one meal left for herself and her son. Miraculously, the elements of that last meal lasted for the duration of the drought.

So?

So what do we learn from these incidents in Elijah's life? We learn plenty, and what we learn can be as challenging to us as Elijah's message was to Ahab and as unusual as a widow giving her last piece of bread to a strange prophet.

First, in this passage of Scripture, we see both Elijah and the widow acting in new, unusual, even risky ways. After all, it's unlikely that Elijah got his breakfast from ravens before this event. But a new circumstance plus guidance from the Lord led him to do that. Then there's the widow. Elijah instructed her to give up a portion of the last bit of food she had for herself and her son. What a terrible choice for her. Should she give food to the prophet, trusting that God would provide? Or should she keep what she had, the sure thing, the last few morsels of food for herself and her son? She took the risk and did a new and unusual thing.

Perhaps we need to learn that the unusual may really be the usual. It's asking too much of our human nature that we should be more surprised when things don't change than when they do change. Even so, it might help us to recognize that change is always occurring and we must be ready to respond in new ways rather than the usual ways.

Second, we learn something in these verses about following God rather than worldly authority. Few people dare to challenge authority, especially when that authority is backed by the force of power and wealth. Most prefer to go along to get along in a conventional manner, rather than appearing too different from their fellow human beings. Even when that authority is not a political leader, such as a king, but rather is the prevailing custom of the day, challenging authority, going against the grain, is not easy for most people.

Whether Elijah's challenge in 17:1 to King Ahab and Ahab's god Baal was easy or not, Elijah did it. He bluntly asserted the priority of God in his life and in the life of his nation. Ahab was king, and Baal was known as the storm god who brought rain. Even so, the true God sent word through Elijah that there would be no rain for three years no matter what the worshipers of Baal and even Ahab the king thought about it. And that was that.

How could Elijah deliver such an unusual message to the king and with such assurance? The lesson text suggests one answer. He ministered in the world of the king, but he lived in the presence of God. That's what true prophets did. They lived in the presence of God, heard

God's message, and spread God's message to all who needed to hear it (see Jeremiah 23:16).

In a brilliant sermon, the twentieth-century German Lutheran preacher Helmut Thíelícke asked why it was that Jesus spoke with such authority. It was not because he was a gifted, dynamic speaker, he said, although perhaps he was. Rather, Jesus spoke to people with such authority and power, the preacher suggested, because Jesus spoke out of his relationship with God. Like Jesus, Elijah disturbed time and challenged authority because he, too, lived in communion with the eternal, with God.[83]

Note that Elijah relied on God and not on the king. This fact tells us something about religion and government in our day. A prime role of religion in relation to government is to be the conscience of the nation, the state, and the city. Religious leaders must not let themselves become so entwined with and so dependent on the state that they dare not deliver God's message. Certainly this is hard in totalitarian states, but it is also difficult in democratic states. The lure of worldly power can be strong.

People who stand in the presence of God and act accordingly in their world are always delivering unusual messages to a world enthralled with power, prestige, and conventional living. Such people somehow are unimpressed with the cultural conventions of getting things, having things, keeping things, and rising constantly up the ladder of success no matter who one steps on on the way up.

Third, we learn something important and life-changing about faith from Elijah. One would have thought that Elijah's delivering the challenging message about rain to King Ahab would have been enough for any person to do for God in a lifetime. But God had even more in mind.

Elijah put himself completely in God's care, trusting only God's ability to provide for his needs. He trusted God's ability to make a little brook provide his water. He trusted that God would send ravens to bring food twice daily. Rather than seeking things for himself, Elijah followed God's instructions and relied on God to provide for his needs.

Such a life is a reversal of the way we usually think life ought to be lived. Living in this manner takes life out of our control. It forces us to follow God's instructions and rely on God for the care we need. This way of life reverses the ordinary expectations we have of ourselves and other people.

Elijah's living this kind of life is just one example of the reversals that appear in this text. His pattern of life reminds us of the kind of life Jesus called us to live in Matthew 6:33, "But strive first for the kingdom of God and his righteousness, and all these things will be given to you as well."

Fourth, we learn that God may ask us to undertake actions that seem questionable, risky, and even impossible. Rather than staying on the east side of the Jordan, Elijah went west to Sidon. Sidon was on the shore of the Mediterranean Sea and was the heartland of Baal worship. Even there, rather than seeking relief from the famine by wining and dining at the table of some wealthy Sidonian, Elijah found a poor widow who had only enough food left for a last meal for herself and her son. Why did Elijah do all of this that seems so out of touch with normal reality? In short, in faith he was obeying God's instructions.

The reversals and the unusual continued with the widow. Focus on her and how she responded. Widows were looked on in Hebrew culture as people deserving special concern. As Israelites heard this story and read this text, they would have thought of the widow as being a pitiable figure (see Ruth 1:20-21). The widow had no man to care for her. Thus her life could be precarious. In addition, the Hebrew Scriptures commanded mercy and special care for widows and condemned mistreatment of widows (Deuteronomy 24:19-21; 26:12; Malachi 3:5).

None of the widow's friends would have blamed her if she had refused to give Elijah something to eat. After all, he was a foreigner, an Israelite. Even worse, the widow had no food to spare. She had only enough food for herself and her son for their next meal, and then there was nothing. Why should she believe Elijah's promise that if she would give what she had, God would see that she had enough?

But in another reversal of what should be expected in the normal course of life, the widow believed. As Elijah had done, "she went and did" (compare 1 Kings 17:15 and 17:5).

Fifth, the text shows us how to respond in faith ourselves. Imagine the widow telling her son what she had just done. *Guess what, son, I just gave some of our last meal to this foreign person I've just met who claims to speak for the God of Israel, not even for our god.* What she had done would have sounded preposterous. Would it work?

It worked! Elijah was right! Because the woman had followed Elijah's instructions and risked all she had, she and her son now had enough to survive the famine (17:15-16).

At first glance the encounter of the widow with Elijah seems like one of those too-good-to-be-true stories that we warn people today not to be taken in by. After all, no one wants to see anyone be taken in by a shyster, especially a religious shyster.

The more we look at it, though, the more the widow's action leads us to see that her obedience is what the life of faith is all about. It's about giving all we have when we don't know for sure. It's about giving 100% commitment when we may be far less than 50% sure. It's about giving when all logic tells us that we should *keep*, if not for ourselves at least for our closest loved ones.

So how can we learn to give in such a manner? Just like Elijah, we learn to give by standing in the presence of God rather than in the presence of the world. We come to understand that all we see is not all there is. We learn that living the eternal life is of more value than accumulating things for this life.

Too, as did the widow, we learn to follow instructions, the most important of which Elijah gave the woman in 17:13: "Do not be afraid." Isn't fear what keeps many people from giving of themselves and their resources? They're afraid they'll run out of what they have and won't have enough for themselves. They'd rather hole up with what they have and try to keep others from getting it than invest what they have in making life better for other people.

So, for example, when the needs of hungry children, even in the United States, are presented, they keep their wallets and purses closed; they might not be able to buy a luxury they want. Or they vote against public school bond elections; after all, why should they care about future generations?

One view of life is that life is short and so we should hold on tightly to what we have; we might lose everything if we don't. Another view of life is that life is short and so we should freely give what we have while we have opportunity; as we give of what we are and have, we might just gain everything that's important and lasting (see Mark 8:34-37).

The widow's response to Elijah offers us the lasting lesson that when God is asking us to do something, we do well to overcome the inner reluctance based on our conventional ideas about safety and security. Reliance on such sure things can keep us from the eternal joy of being surprised by God's blessings.

A tiny woman leaves her post at a high school in Kolkata to minister to the sick and dying on the streets. We know her now as Mother Teresa and honor her life and her memory.[84]

A couple feel called to missionary service in a difficult setting. They sell their home and their possessions and leave behind many of the things a materialistic culture says they ought not even think of doing without. When we see them next, somehow they seem happier and more fulfilled than we ever remember.

A young man puts himself in danger over and over in the segregated South. He is beaten severely more than once. He is jailed more than forty times during this era and five times more as a member of the United States House of Representatives. He does it all in the spirit of Christ for the dignity and worth of his fellow human beings. John Lewis did the unusual, and his life continues to be a beacon of hope.[85]

We hear the message of such folks and wonder what to make of it. Maybe we ought to listen and learn from them, asking ourselves how we can respond to opportunities to give of ourselves and our resources in fresh and different ways. Perhaps we, too, will know God's blessings in surprising ways. One question this lesson calls us to ask is, *How can I give of myself and what I have more freely when my first inclination is to keep for myself?*

Dietrich Bonhoeffer, the German theologian and Christian leader, wrote these words during his imprisonment by Hitler in the closing days of

World War II. He would not be freed except by execution. I can hear not only Bonhoeffer but also Elijah, Mother Teresa, John Lewis, and other faithful Christians in these words. Bonhoeffer wrote:[86]

> Choose and do what is right,
> not what fancy takes,
> not weighing the possibilities, but
>   bravely grasping the real,
> not in the flight of ideas, but only
>   in action is there freedom.
> Come away from your anxious
>   hesitations
> into the storm of events
> carried by God's command and
>   your faith alone.

33.
1 Samuel 1:4-20; 2:1-10
A Hope, a Prayer, a Promise, a Praise

Proper 28 (33):
Twenty-Fifth Sunday after Pentecost

In the midst of the story of ancient Israel with its tales of judges, wars, prophets, and, later, kings, we find a little gem about a woman who wanted a baby but was unable to have one. It's the story of her anguish and her disappointment and then of what she did to overcome her sadness in what she was experiencing. It's a story about hope, about prayer, about a promise, and then about praise for God's blessings.

Perhaps it's in the stories of seemingly small happenings like this that we most often experience the presence of God. It's altogether possible and even likely that every person experiences in some way what the woman in this story experienced. That's so whether we are men or women. We all have hopes and dreams, To understand these experiences and how they apply to our faith, let's give careful attention to what happened to this woman named Hannah.

First, though, a brief comment about the book in which her story appears. The two books of

Samuel in our Bibles begin with a surprising little word in the Hebrew. It's the word *and*.[87] That little word serves as a reminder that 1 and 2 Samuel are part of a continued story.

In the Hebrew Bible, the canonical book that precedes 1 Samuel is the Book of Judges. So the story is continued from the Book of Judges. These books—Joshua, Judges, Samuel, and Kings—comprise the part of the Hebrew canon called the former prophets. The books tell the story of Israel's rise and then, centuries later, its fall. They were written not just to record history but to tell why the nation's fall occurred. They are books of theology and as much as they are books of history.

The last verse of the Book of Judges precedes immediately this passage in 1 Samuel. That verse reads, "In those days there was no king in Israel; all the people did what was right in their own eyes" (Judges 21:25). That's the situation in which we find this woman and the little family of which she was a part. They lived in a mixed-up time.

Despair (1:1-8)

There generally is the darkness of despair before there is the light of hope. It may be only a little time of darkness, but it is there. That was the case with Hannah.

For Hannah, the despair was great. She wanted a child but had been unable to have one. This lack was a source of great sorrow and despair, particularly for a Hebrew wife. Hannah not only wanted the joy of a baby but also to fulfill what she felt was her destiny—to bear a child for her husband. Many women today can resonate with Hannah and her feelings. This lack can be a source of despair for women who want to have a child but have not been able to for one reason or another.

So we should not read the comment at the end of verse 2, "Hannah had no children," as just a statement of fact. The fact that she had no children was burdensome and troubling. This reality brought Hannah great despair.

Even the love of Hannah's husband, Elkanah, could not make up for this lack of a baby. Hannah was likely Elkanah's first wife. Likely he had taken a second wife mainly to ensure that the family lineage continued.[88] Even so, "he loved her," and he treated Hannah with great respect, kindness, and love (1 Samuel 1:5, 8). He made sure that she received an extra portion of food when they went to the tabernacle to make an offering. One of the offerings in the sacrificial system was a meal in which the participants gave a portion to the priests and then shared in a family and community feast of the remainder (see (Leviticus 3:1-17; 7:11-19). This was a thanksgiving offering, sometimes called a peace or fellowship or "well-being" offering.[89] Even her husband Elkanah's kindness and love were not enough to move Hannah beyond despair, however.

Also, it did not help when someone said something like this to childless Hannah: *Cheer up and just deal with it; your inability to have a child is the Lord's will.* Probably plenty of pious people said of Hannah, in whispered tones, that "the LORD had closed her womb" (1 Sam.1:5). Perhaps Hannah felt that even God was against her.

A Hope , a Prayer, and a Promise (1:9-11)

Likely Hannah had been doing all she could to get pregnant before this incident occurred. Do I have to explain all the details of what she had been doing? Yes, she and Elkanah were trying. Anyway, this incident at the tabernacle in Shiloh brought her despair to a focus and a result in hope expressed in a prayer and a promise within that prayer.

At Shiloh, Hannah prayed again for a child, "a male child" (1:11). Although women could inherit family property (see Numbers 36), passing along the inheritance was easier and more acceptable if the child were male. Perhaps more important, only a boy would fit within the promise Hannah was making to rear the child as a nazirite. To be a nazirite in ancient Israel was to be set aside to God in a special way. "He shall drink neither wine nor intoxicants, and no razor shall touch his head" (1 Sam. 1:11; see also Num. 6:1-8).

Affirmation of the Prayer (1:12-18)

Eli, the priest, was observing the woman as she prayed. He saw that "only her lips moved, but her voice was not heard" (1 Sam. 1:13). So he was concerned. He thought Hannah might be drunk and accused her of it.

When Hannah explained her thoughts and feelings, Eli accepted what she said. He then told her, "Go in peace; the God of Israel grant the petition you have made to him" (1:17). In essence, he affirmed her prayer and joined her in her petition.

God's Answer (1:19-20)

God did answer Hannah's prayer. But the answer was not God's alone. "Elkanah knew his wife Hannah" (1:19). Of course, "knew" is a familiar euphemism—a polite word—for sexual intercourse.

Hooray! A miracle occurred! The miracle occurred in the natural course of life, but God made it happen. Isn't there something miraculous about a baby even though you know where babies come from?

A new father wrote a little poem to express his feelings about the birth of his child. This was from the time when fathers were not allowed in the delivery room. This new father, Dr. Henlee Barnette, a seminary professor of mine long years ago, wrote:

> At last the nurse with bundle small
> Appeared before me in the hall.
> She said, "You have a baby boy."
> I gazed upon that little life with mingled
> awe
> and glee.
> And thought that God himself had come
> down
> to shake hands with me.[90]

Verse 19 puts it like this: " . . . the LORD remembered her." This biblical expression means that the Lord *paid attention to her to meet her need.* So "remembered" in this verse doesn't mean that the Lord had forgotten her. Perhaps it appeared to Hannah that the Lord had forgotten her. He hadn't, though. He remembered her all along.[91] Now the Lord acted to meet her need and fulfill her hope.

So Hannah had a baby boy. Her naming him Samuel showed that she was keeping her promise to God, even as God had fulfilled his promise to her.

Keeping the Promise (1:21-28)

Hannah fulfilled her promise to the Lord. She nursed and reared the child until he was weaned. A Hebrew mother generally nursed her child until the child was about three years old (see 2 Maccabees 7:27).[92]

A Song of Praise (2:1-10)

Chapter 2 begins with Hannah's song of praise. It's a song expressing her praise of God and her hopes for her child.

It's often been noted that Mary's song in Luke 1:46-56, the Magnificat, has a relationship with Hannah's song. Compare especially Luke 1:52-54 and 1 Samuel 2:4-5.

Joining in Hope, Prayer, Commitment, and Praise

Here are some thoughts about how Hannah's experience might speak to us. First, it speaks to us about family.

No matter how old a child gets, we never forget that we are the parents, do we? That includes the blessings of parenthood as well as the tragedies sometimes associated with parenthood.

Too, it's our families that mean the most to us when we look back on our lives—the difficulties as well as the joys. Admiral Richard E. Byrd was renowned for his polar expeditions, especially in Antartica. Most of this was in the first half of the twentieth century.[93] On one of his expeditions, he decided he would spend the long polar night alone. He was living in a little shack buried in the snow several miles from the base camp. Unfortunately, something went wrong with the stove so that the fumes were poisoning him. For long weeks, he lay in his sleeping bag, thinking he would never survive. He did survive, and he wrote a book about the experience. Its title is *Alone.* In his book *Alone,* he told how in those weeks about what his mind was focused on. His list of professional achievements was long. He had even been given the Congressional Medal of Honor. But that was not what his mind was focused on as he contemplated the end of his life. His mind was focused on his family. He said,

> At the end only two things really matter to a man, regardless of who he is; and they

are the affection and understanding of his family. Anything and everything else he creates are insubstantial. . . . [94]

All of life, all of history, begins with parents who have a child. That's so with us. Even if we don't have children, we likely know the importance of family. That was so with Hannah. That was so with ancient Israel.

Hannah's experience also speaks to us about hope and about prayer. Some years ago Dr. Elizabeth Kubler-Ross, a physician working with terminally ill patients, came to the thought that there were stages in which these patients came to terms with their approaching death—denial, anger, bargaining, depression, acceptance. She developed and explained these stages in her classic book, *On Death and Dying*. These stages seemed so helpful that over time they have been broadened to be understood as stages of grief over the loss of pretty much anything important. [95]

Perhaps we can see in Hannah's experience something similar about hope. At least we can see that Hannah went through despair, hope, prayer, commitment to God, acting in accord with her prayer, and then praise for God's answer.

Considering such stages might help us as we deal with the despairing times of our lives. An unusually personal article appeared in the New York *Times* the day before Thanksgiving in 2020, which was a hard year for just about everybody. [96] It was by Meghan, the Duchess of Sussex. You know, Meghan Markle, whose husband is Prince Harry. The article is titled, "The Losses We

Share." In the article, she told about the dark time when she experienced a miscarriage. She also told of how she was helped immensely when a journalist asked her in a friendly, concerned way, "Are you ok?"

Here are some questions we might ask ourselves today. Is there someone you know who would be helped if you asked, *Are you ok?*

Perhaps that person is you. Are you ok? Where do you need hope today?

Hannah's experience also calls us to consider something about prayer. What would your prayer life say about you and what you most desire?

What promise would you make to the Lord in connection with your prayer? I'm not inclined to say that you should bargain with the Lord in your prayer, even though that appears to be what Hannah did. My own thought is that if you believe the Lord wants you to do something, you should just do it. Don't try to do a quid pro quo. Don't make it a transaction. Just do it. You might say, *Well, it looks like Hannah bargained with God.* Yes, but we don't see that when we get to Jesus in the New Testament. So I say, just pray, act in faith, and trust the Lord.

Here's another question to consider: What action do you need to take to work with God in answering your prayer?

Here's another: What praise is due the Lord from you for how he has already helped you?

One more thing. The article by Meghan, Duchess of Sussex, ends with these two lines:

Are we ok?
We will be.

Hannah would agree. She also would say that it all begins with hope.

About the Author

Ross West has had a varied career in publishing, writing, and preaching. A friend once asked him how many careers he had had anyway. To Ross, it seems like one, but he can understand how others see more than one. He has served churches in New York, Kentucky, Arkansas, Virginia, Louisiana, and Georgia. He also has been involved in a ministry of writing and publishing in both secular and religious venues.

Through his career in publishing, he has led in producing hundreds of Bible studies and has written numerous articles, Bible studies, and sermons. His most recent place of ministry was as publisher of BaptistWay Press®97 in Dallas, Texas. Prior to that he served as an editor and then manager of an adult Sunday School editorial section at the Baptist Sunday School Board, Nashville, Tennessee, and as director of Creative Services for the national organization of the Boy Scouts of America. For a number of years, he has had his own writing and publishing consulting business, Positive Difference Communications.

In addition to this book, Ross is the author of *How to Be Happier in the Job You Sometimes Can't Stand; Seven Words to Live By; The Christmas to Remember; Living in the Meanwhile;*

Guidance for a Good Life; Grief and Hope; Reading the Bible Jesus Read; and *Go to Work and Take Your Faith Too!* as well as these additional volumes in the Understanding the New Testament series:; *Understanding the Gospel of Matthew; Understanding the Gospel of Mark; Understanding the Gospel of Luke; Understanding the Gospel of John; Understanding the Book of Acts; Understanding 1 Corinthians; Understanding 2 Corinthians; Understanding the Letter to the Galatians; Understanding the Letter to the Ephesians; Understanding the Letter to the Philippians; Understanding the Letters to the Colossians and Philemon; Understanding 1 and 2 Thessalonians; Understanding the Book of Hebrews; Understanding the Book of James; Understanding 1, 2, and 3 John;* and *Understanding the Book of Revelation.* He is co-author of another (*Teaching Adults the Bible,* out of print).[98] Among his published writing, he has had sermons published in three annual editions of *The Abingdon Preaching Annual.*

Ross served for ten years on the Committee on the Uniform Series, the interdenominational group that plans the International Sunday School Lesson Series under the auspices of the National Council of Churches.[99] Also, through his participation in the Baptist World Alliance, he produced Bible study materials for two meetings of the Baptist World Congress. He has led numerous Bible studies in churches through the years, and he has taught college Bible courses as an adjunct professor. He has also led conferences across the nation on teaching the Bible. His seminary education includes the degree of Doctor of Ministry in Biblical Studies, focused on studies in the Greek New Testament.

For Additional Copies

Additional copies of the print edition of this book as well as a Kindle edition are available on amazon.com. My author page lists my books, print as well as Kindle.

Go to "Books" on amazon.com, do a search for "Ross West," and click on my author page. Or use this web address as a shortcut: www.amazon.com/author/ross_west.

Index of Scripture Texts

Mark 6:1-13. *A Pattern for Christian Living*
16. Proper 9 (14):
Sixth Sunday after Pentecost

Mark 7:1-8, 14-15, 21-23.
Clean Hands or Pure Hearts
20. Proper 17 (22):
Fourteenth Sunday after Pentecost

Mark 8:27-38. *The Right Place for You*
21. Proper 19 (24):
Sixteenth Sunday after Pentecost

Mark 10:35-45. *A New Standard of Success*
22. Proper 24 (29):
Twenty-First Sunday after Pentecost

Mark 12:28-34. *Where It All Begins*
24. Proper 26 (31):
Twenty-Third Sunday after Pentecost

Mark 14:3-9, 22-25, 32-36.
Some Things Can't Wait
6. Liturgy of the Passion:
Sixth Sunday in Lent

Mark 16:1-8. *The Reality of the Resurrection*
8. Resurrection of the Lord: Easter Day

John 3:14-21. *Your Spiritual Survival Kit*
5. Fourth Sunday in Lent

John 13:1-17, 31b-35.
What Life Is Meant to Be Like
7. Maundy Thursday

Endnotes

Introduction

[1] The details of the Revised Common Lectionary can be found here: http://lectionary.library.vanderbilt.edu. Accessed 7/27/17.

1. Matthew 1:18-25. *The Miracles of Christmas.* Fourth Sunday of Advent

[2] "O Come, All Ye Faithful," Latin hymn; ascribed to John Francis Wade, translated by Frederick Oakeley.

2. Ephesians 1:3-14. *What God Is Up To.* Second Sunday after Christmas Day

[3] See http://curious.astro.cornell.edu/the-universe/galaxies and http://blogs.discovermagazine.com/crux/2012/10/10/how-many-galaxies-are-there-in-the-universe-the-redder-we-look-the-more-we-see/#.VYmy52C_3rw. Both accessed 7/27/17.

[4] https://www.space.com/26078-how-many-stars-are-there.html. Accessed 7/28/17.

[5] http://curious.astro.cornell.edu/the-universe/the-milky-way. Accessed 7/27/17.

[6] http://oscar.go.com/blogs/oscar-history/2014-86th-academy-award-winners. Accessed 7/27/17.

3. 1 Samuel 3:1-20. *Listening.* Second Sunday after the Epiphany

[7] https://www.britannica.com/biography/Steven-Spielberg. Accessed 12/4/2020.

[8] See https://www.stpauls.co.uk/history-collections/the-collections/collections-highlights/the-light-of-the-world. Accessed 12/4/2020.

[9] Ben F. Philbeck, Jr., "1—2 Samuel," *The Broadman Bible Commentary,* vol. 3 (Nashville, TN: Broadman Press, 1970), 19.

[10] Roger L. Omanson, John E. Ellington, "1 Samuel," *UBS Handbooks* (New York: United Bible Societies, 2001), comments on 1 Samuel 3:6-7.

[11] Matt Emerson, "Steven Spielberg: Listen for the Whisper," *America: The Jesuit Review* (December 9, 2014). See https://www.americamagazine.org/content/ignatian-educator/steven-spielberg-listen-whisper. Accessed 12/4/2020.

[12] Words by Frances Havergal. See https://hymnary.org/text/lord_speak_to_me_that_i_may_speak. Accessed 12/4/2020.

4. Mark 2:13-22. *Follow the Leader.* Eighth Sunday after the Epiphany

[13] Dorothy L. Sayers, *The Man Born to Be King: A Play-Cycle on the Life of Our Lord and Saviour Jesus Christ* (New York: Harper and Brothers, 1943), 109-110.

[14] Gordon Allport, *The Individual and His Religion* (New York: The Macmillan Company, 1950), 33-34.

[15] Howard K. Batson, *Common-Sense Church Growth* (Macon, Georgia: Smyth and Helwys Publishing, Inc., 1999), 136-137.

5. John 3:14-21. *Your Spiritual Survival Kit.* Fourth Sunday in Lent

[16] For an evangelistic sermon on John 3:16, see Billy Graham, "Why God Allows Suffering and War," in *20 Centuries of Great Preaching*, ed. Clyde E. Fant, Jr., and William M. Pinson, Jr., vol. XII (Waco, TX: Word Books, Publisher, 1971), 312-320.

6. Mark 14:3-9, 22-25, 32-36. *Some Things Can't Wait.* Liturgy of the Passion: Sixth Sunday in Lent

[17] William Shakespeare, *Julius Caesar*, Act IV, Scene 3.

[18] Billy Graham, *Just As I Am: the Autobiography of Billy Graham* (New York: HarperCollins Worldwide, 1997), 720.

[19] Leonard Sweet, *SoulTsunami* (Grand Rapids, Michigan: Zondervan Publishing House, 1999), 98.

[20] Sweet, *SoulTsunami*, 275, citing John M. Buchanan, "Give It All," Fourth Presbyterian Church, Chicago, Illinois (23 Oct 1994):1, quoting Erma Bombeck.

7. John 13:1-17, 31b-35. *What Life Is Meant to Be Like.* **Maundy Thursday**
[21] William Barclay, *The Revelation of John*, vol. 2, second edition, The Daily Study Bible (Philadelphia: The Westminster Press, 1960), 31.

8. Mark 16:1-8. *The Reality of the Resurrection.* **Resurrection of the Lord: Easter Day**
[22] For an insightful sermon on this passage, see Helmut Thielicke, "Time and Eternity," in *20 Centuries of Great Preaching*, ed. Clyde E. Fant, Jr., and William M. Pinson, Jr., vol. XII (Waco, TX: Word Books, Publisher, 1971), 269-276.

9. 1 John 1:1—2:2. *What Is Christianity?* **Second Sunday of Easter**
[23] Keith Miller and Bruce Larson, *The Edge of Adventure: An Experiment in Faith* (Waco, Texas: Word books, Publisher, 1974), 29. See also the folk song by the Kingston Singers, "Desert Peter," by Billy Edd Wheeler at http://www.oldielyrics.com/lyrics/the_kingston_trio/desert_p ete.html. Accessed 7/27/17.

13. Ezekiel 37:1-14. *Hope in Death Valley.* **Day of Pentecost**
[24] By James and Rosamund Johnson. http://lyricsplayground.com/alpha/songs/d/demdrybones.sht ml. Accessed 7/29/17.

14. Isaiah 6:1-8. *Just Say Yes.* **Trinity Sunday: First Sunday after Pentecost**
[25] For meaningful insights on this Scripture passage, see Frederick Buechner, "The Calling of Voices," sermon 6 in *Secrets in the Dark: A Life in Sermons* (New York: Harper Collins Publishers, 2009).

15. 1 Samuel 8:4-20. *Be Wise about What You Want.* Proper 5 (10): Second Sunday after Pentecost

[26] https://hymnary.org/text/come_thou_fount_of_every_blessing. Accessed 12/8/2020.

[27] John I. Durham, "Psalms," *The Broadman Bible Commentary,* vol. 4 (Nashville, TN: Broadman Press, 1971), 167.

[28] See the comments on these psalms in John I. Durham, "Psalms," *The Broadman Bible Commentary,* vol. 4.

[29] Ben F. Philbeck, Jr., *The Broadman Bible Commentary,* vol. 3 (Nashville, TN: Broadman Press, 1970), 31.

[30] Shimon Bar-Efrat, revised by Marc Zvi Brettler, "1 Samuel," *The Jewish Study Bible,* 2nd ed. (New York: Oxford University Press, 2014), comments on 1 Samuel 8:18.

[31] https://www.britannica.com/biography/Saint-Teresa-of-Avila. Accessed 12/13/2020.

16. Mark 4:26-34. *More Than Meets the Eye.* Proper 6 (11): Third Sunday after Pentecost

[32] Helmut Thielicke, *The Waiting Father,* trans. and with an introduction by John Doberstein (New York: Harper & Row Publishers, 1959), 89.

[33] Reuel L. Howe, *How to Stay Younger While Growing Older* (Waco, Texas: Word Books, Publisher, 1974), 120.

17. 1 Samuel 17:57—18:16. *Facing the Green-Eyed Monster.* Proper 7 (12): Fourth Sunday after Pentecost

[34] William Shakespeare, *Othello,* Act 3, Scene 3, lines 165-167.

[35] Thomas Aquinas, *The Summa Theologica,* Second Part of the Second Part, #36, citing Damascene, *De Fide Orth.* Ii. 14. See https://www.ccel.org/a/aquinas/summa/SS/SS036.html#SSQ36OUTP1, accessed 12/31/2020.

[36] Lester Flatt, "I'm Going to Sleep with One Eye Open." https://www.azlyrics.com/lyrics/dollyparton/imgonnasleepwithoneeyeopen.html. Accessed 1/1/2021.

[37] Adapted from my book *Go to Work and Take Your Faith Too!* (Macon, GA: Smyth and Helwys—Peake Road Press, 1997), 139-140.

[38] James Mulholland, *Praying Like Jesus: The Lord's Prayer in a Culture of Prosperity* (San Francisco: HarperSanFrancisco, 2001), 44.

18. Mark 5:21-43. *Victory in Jesus?* Proper 8 (13): Fifth Sunday after Pentecost

[39] Helmut Thielicke, *The Waiting Father: The Parables of Jesus*, trans. and with an introduction by John W. Doberstein (New York: Harper & Row, Publishers, 1959), 88, italics in original.

[40] James Weldon Johnson, *God's Trombones: Seven Negro Sermons in Verse*, drawings by Aaron Douglas, lettering by C. B. Falls (New York: The Viking Press, 1961), 27-30.

[41] Joseph B. Underwood, *By Love Compelled* (Nashville, Tennessee: Broadman Press, 1966), 39.

19. Mark 6:1-13. *A Pattern for Christian Living.* Proper 9 (14): Sixth Sunday after Pentecost

[42] James L. Sullivan, "A Different Book," *Facts and Trends* (September 1973): 3.

20. 2 Corinthians 12:1-10. *Your Greatest Strength.* Proper 9 (14): Sixth Sunday after Pentecost

[43] O. Hobart Mowrer, "How to Talk About Your Troubles," Walden Howard and the editors of *Faith at Work*, compilers, *Groups That Work* (Grand Rapids, MI: Zondervan Publishing House, 1967), 109.

[44] http://www.nytimes.com/2015/09/11/us/politics/joe-biden-in-colbert-interview-expresses-doubts-about-bid-for-president.html?_r=0. Accessed 7/27/17.

[45] Bryan Stevenson, *Just Mercy: A Story of Justice and Redemption* (New York: Random House Publishing Group, 2014), 288-289.

[46] Stevenson, *Just Mercy*, 289-290.

21. 2 Samuel 7:1-14a. A Secure Future for God's People. Proper 11 (16): Eighth Sunday after Pentecost

[47] Bruce C. Birch, "1 and 2 Samuel," *The New Interpreter's Bible*, volume II (Nashville, Tennessee: Abingdon Press, 1998), 1254. See also A. A. Anderson, *2 Samuel*, Word Biblical Commentary, volume 11 (Dallas, Texas: Word Books, Publisher, 1989), 112.

[48] Walter Brueggemann, *First and Second Samuel*, Interpretation: A Bible Commentary for Teaching and Preaching (Louisville: John Knox Press, 1990), see on 2 Samuel 7:1-17.

[49] Roger L. Omanson, John E. Ellington, "2 Samuel," *UBS Handbooks* (New York: United Bible Societies, 2001), comments on 2 Samuel 7:2.

[50] "Trust and Obey," words by John H. Sammis.

22. 2 Samuel 11:26—12:13a. When the Truth Comes Out. Proper 13 (18): Tenth Sunday after Pentecost

[51] Sir Walter Scott (1771-1832), *Marmion*, Canto VI, Stanza XVII.

[52] In a letter to Bishop Mandell Creighton from John Emerich Edward Dalberg, Lord Acton. https://www.smithsonianmag.com/science-nature/why-power-corrupts-37165345/ and https://www.phrases.org.uk/meanings/absolute-power-corrupts-absolutely.html. Both accessed 01/15/2021.

23. Ephesians 4:1-16. *Toward a Worthy Life.* Proper 13 (18): Tenth Sunday after Pentecost

[53] http://www.nytimes.com/2015/04/12/opinion/sunday/david-brooks-the-moral-bucket-list.html?_r=0. Accessed 6/15/2015. See also David Brooks, *The Road to Character* (New York: Random House, 2015), Kindle edition location 65.

[54] http://www.metrolyrics.com/its-hard-to-be-humble-lyrics-mac-davis.html. Accessed 7/28/17.

[55] See the poem, "You Tell On Yourself," at http://www.poemhunter.com/poem/tell-on-yourself/. Accessed 6/15/2015.

[56] Kenneth Chafin, *The Reluctant Witness* (Nashville, TN: Broadman Press, 1974), 137-138.

[57] See the poem, "Christ Has No Hands But Our Hands," by Annie Johnson Flint, as a hymn text at http://www.scoreexchange.com/scores/84363.html. Accessed 7/27/17.

24. 2 Samuel 18:5-9, 15, 31-33. *Nightmare in the Daytime.* Proper 14 (19): Eleventh Sunday after Pentecost

[58] 1 Chronicles 10—29 provides a parallel account of David's reign. The tragic events of 2 Samuel 11—1 Kings 2 are not mentioned there, however. The Books of Chronicles are concerned not so much with why the exile happened but with what next after the exile. The *what next* would include David as the most revered king of Israel and the prototype of the messiah.

[59] O. Henry. *Trimmed Lamp, and Other Stories of the Four Million* [with Biographical Introduction] (Kindle Locations 2489-2490). Neeland Media LLC. Kindle Edition.

25. 1 Kings 19:4-8. *Finding the Way Out and Up.* Proper 14 (19): Eleventh Sunday after Pentecost

[60] See http://www.mayoclinic.org/diseases-conditions/depression/home/ovc-20321449 for more information. Accessed 7/24/17.

[61] See also https://suicidepreventionlifeline.org. Call 1-800-273-8255. Accessed 7/27/17.

[62] See https://www.stpauls.co.uk/history-collections/the-collections/collections-highlights/the-light-of-the-world. Accessed 12/4/2020.

27. Mark 8:27-38. *The Right Place for You.* Proper 19 (24): Sixteenth Sunday after Pentecost

[63] Carl R. Rogers, *On Becoming a Person* (Boston: Houghton Mifflin Company, 1961), 108.

[64] *Macbeth*, Act 5, Scene 5, lines 24-28. See http://www.shakespeare-online.com/plays/macbeth_5_5.html. Accessed 7/27/17.

[65] E. Stanley Jones, *A Song of Ascents: A Spiritual Autobiography* (Nashville: Abingdon Press, 1968), 31.
[66] John A. Redhead, *Guidance from Men of God* (New York: Abingdon Press, 1965), 115.
[67] "Where He Leads Me," words by E. W. Blandy. http://nethymnal.org/htm/w/h/e/wherehlm.htm. Accessed 7/26/2017.
[68] Joseph B. Underwood, *By Love Compelled* (Nashville, Tennessee: Broadman Press, 1966), 107-108.
[69] Frederick Buechner, *Wishful Thinking* (New York: Harper & Row Publishers, 1993), 107.

28. Mark 10:35-45. *A New Standard of Success*. Proper 24 (29): Twenty-First Sunday after Pentecost

[70] Lloyd J. Ogilvie, *Life Without Limits: The Message of Mark's Gospel* (Waco, Texas: Word Books, 1975), 190.
[71] Samuel M. Shoemaker, *And Thy Neighbor* (Waco, Texas: Word Books, 1967), 18.

29. Job 42:1-6, 10-17. *A Problem for Faith*. Proper 25 (30): Twenty-Second Sunday after Pentecost

[72] From G. A. Studdert Kennedy, "Faith," *The Unutterable Beauty: The Collected Poetry of G. A. Studdert Kennedy* (London: Hodder and Stoughton, 1927).

30. Mark 12:28-34. *Where It All Begins*. Proper 26 (31). Twenty-Third Sunday after Pentecost

[73] *Time* (December 31, 1999). http://content.time.com/time/magazine/article/0,9171,993017,00.html. Accessed 7/27/17.

31. Hebrews 9:24-28. *Can Things Ever Be All Right Again?* Proper 27 (32): Twenty-Fourth Sunday after Pentecost

[74] Gerald Kennedy, "The Trouble with Religion," *20 Centuries of Great Preaching*, ed. Clyde E. Fant, Jr., and William M. Pinson, Jr., vol. XII (Waco, TX: Word Books, Publishers, 1971), 153.

[75] Gilbert Keith Chesterton, *Wit and Wisdom of G. K. Chesterton* (New York: Dodd, Mead, and Company, 1911), 192.

[76] Three different Greek words are used in this passage for this same idea, but several English translation use a form of the word *appearing* to translate these Greek words (see NRSV, NIV, KJV).

[77] Louisa Fletcher, "The Land of Beginning Again." See http://writersalmanac.publicradio.org/index.php?date=2013/05/10. Accessed 7/27/17.

[78] "What a Friend We Have in Jesus," words by Joseph M. Scriven. See http://library.timelesstruths.org/music/What_a_Friend_We_Have_in_Jesus/. Accessed 7/27/17.

32. 1 Kings 17:1-16, *Open to the Unusual,* Twenty-Fourth Sunday after Pentecost

[79] This meditation is adapted from my lesson comments in *The New International Lesson Annual 2000-2001* (Nashville, TN: Abingdon Press, 2000), 379-384.

[80] Karl Albrecht, *Brain Power: Learning to Improve Your Thinking Skills* (Englewood Cliffs, NJ: Prentice-Hall, Inc., 1980), 34.

[81] S.J. DeVries, *I Kings*, Word Biblical Commentary (Waco, Texas: Word Books, Publisher, 1985), 216.

[82] John Gray, *I and II Kings*, The Old Testament Library, Second, Fully Revised, Edition (Philadelphia: The Westminster Press, 1970), 377.

[83] Helmut Thielicke, *The Waiting Father*, trans. with an introduction by John W. Doberstein (New York: Harper & Row, Publishers, 1959), 89.

[84] "Mother Teresa." *Encyclopedia Britannica,* September 1, 2020. https://www.britannica.com/biography/Mother-Teresa. Accessed 02/04/2021.

[85] Jon Meacham, *His Truth Is Marching On: John Lewis and the Power of Hope* (New York: Random House, 2020).

[86] Dietrich Bonhoeffer, Edwin Robertson, ed. and trans, *Dietrich Bonhoeffer's Prison Poems* (New York: HarperCollins, 2005), 73.

33. 1 Samuel 1:4-20; 2:1-10. *A Hope, a Prayer, a Promise, a Praise.* Proper 28 (33): Twenty-Fifth Sunday after Pentecost

[87] Roger L. Omanson, John E. Ellington, "1 Samuel," *UBS Handbooks* (New York: United Bible Societies, 2001), comments on 1 Samuel 1:1-8.

[88] Roger L. Omanson, John E. Ellington, "1 Samuel," *UBS Handbooks*, comments on 1 Samuel 1:2

[89] Roger L. Omanson, John E. Ellington, "1 Samuel," *UBS Handbooks,* comments on 1 Samuel 1:5.

[90] Poem by Henlee Barnette.

[91] Roger L. Omanson, John E. Ellington, "1 Samuel," *UBS Handbooks*, comments on 1 Samuel 1:19

[92] Roger L. Omanson, John E. Ellington, "1 Samuel," *UBS Handbooks*, comments on 1 Samuel 1:22, 24

[93] https://www.britannica.com/biography/Richard-E-Byrd/Byrds-accomplishments. Accessed 11/28/2020.

[94] Richard E. Byrd, *Alone: The Classic Polar Adventure* (New York: G.P. Putnam's Sons, 1938), 179.

[95] See https://www.mcgill.ca/oss/article/health-history/its-time-let-five-stages-grief-die. Accessed 11/28/2020.

[96] Meghan, the Ducchess of Sussex, "The Losses We Share," *New York Times*, November 25, 2020. https://www.nytimes.com/2020/11/25/opinion/meghan-markle-miscarriage.html?searchResultPosition=1/. Accessed 11/25/2020.

About the Author

[97] www.baptistwaypress.org. Accessed 3/29/2020.

[98] Go to www.amazon.com, Do a search on amazon for any of the books listed in "Also by Ross West" on pages 2 -3 of this book. Or use this web address for a shortcut: www.amazon.com/author/ross_west Accessed 3/29/2020.

[99] http://www.ncccusa.org/news/120326uniformlessons.html. Accessed 3/29/2020.

Printed in Great Britain
by Amazon